Some managers assume new positions with ease, getting along with superiors and subordinates, effectively learning the ropes, and eventually "owning" the job. Others fail miserably. *The Dynamics Of Taking Charge* asks "why?"

In this comparative study of seventeen successful and unsuccessful managerial transitions, (including division presidents, general managers, and functional managers), Harvard Business School professor John J. Gabarro isolates specific factors, ranging from prior industry experience, support from superiors, and effective interpersonal relationships, which account for managerial success. He ably guides the reader through the five predictable stages that new managers go through in taking charge of their responsibilities: taking hold, immersion, reshaping, consolidation, and refinement, as well as the learning and action issues they face at each stage. Gabarro also describes how managers accomplish the organizational and interpersonal work that leads to successful transitions.

The findings in *The Dynamics Of Taking Charge* hold significant implications for succession planning and career development. By documenting the effects of prior industry and functional experience, Gabarro punctures the myth of the "all-purpose manager" who can succeed in any situation. Instead, he demonstrates how managers' prior experience greatly influences the manner in which they take charge, on what areas they focus, and how successful they will be in mastering a new situation. At the same time, however, a manager's career development may be enhanced by a position that stretches his expertise. Top management needs to weigh these competing considerations in making its appointments—but Gabarro also urges management to allow new managers the time to work through the entire taking-charge process.

The average executive will make from three to nine job changes by the time he or she is fifty. *The Dynamics Of Taking Charge* has important implications for effective managerial job succession not only for those facing new responsibilities, but also for those top managers who want to develop seasoned successors.

John J. Gabarro is professor of organizational behavior and human resource management at Harvard Business School. He is coauthor of *Interpersonal Behavior* and *Managing Behavior In Organizations,* and is the author of numerous articles.

The Dynamics of Taking Charge

The Dynamics of Taking Charge

89-026

John J. Gabarro

HARVARD BUSINESS SCHOOL PRESS
BOSTON, MASSACHUSETTS

HARVARD BUSINESS SCHOOL PRESS

Tables 1-4, 3-1, 3-3 and Figures 2-1, 2-2, C-3 reprinted by permission of the
Harvard Business Review "When a New Manager Takes Charge," by John J.
Gabarro, May–June 1985. Copyright © 1985 by the President and Fellows of
Harvard College; all rights reserved. Figures A-2, A-3, C-1, C-2, C-4 from
Course Development & Research Profile, 1983. Copyright © 1983 by the President and Fellows of Harvard College, reprinted by permission.

Library of Congress Cataloging-in-Publication Data

Gabarro, John J.
  The dynamics of taking charge.

  Bibliography: p. 189
  Includes index.
  1. Industrial management.   2. Corporate planning.
3. Executives.   4. Personnel management.   I. Title.
HD38.G225   1987   658.4   86-25624
ISBN 0-87585-137-6

CONTENTS

PREFACE

This book reports the findings of a research project on managers taking charge of organizations in management successions. It is different from most books on management succession in that it focuses on the taking-charge process itself rather than on the conditions that lead up to a succession. It also differs from most books on the topic because it focuses on general management and upper-level functional successions rather than on CEO successions.

The purpose of the book is to describe the organizational and interpersonal dynamics of how managers take charge: the stages of learning and action that characterize the taking-charge process; the situational and personal background factors that bear on the process; and the patterns of behavior that distinguish successful transitions from those that fail. Although the presentation of the findings is mainly descriptive, the book also draws implications of a normative nature for the organizational and interpersonal work of taking charge as well as for such pre-succession activities as selection, career development, problem-scoping, and transition management.

With these goals in mind, the book is aimed at three audiences: (1) senior-level executives who are in the process of taking charge of general management or upper-level functional assignments; (2) senior corporate officers and corporate personnel staff who are concerned with succession planning and transition management; and (3) fellow academicians and researchers interested in the problems of executive succession and effective leadership.

The findings are based on a series of field studies of seventeen management successions involving division general managers, subsidiary presidents, group executives, and division-level functional executives in marketing, manufacturing, and service operations. The successions studied occurred in fourteen firms in the United States and Europe. The findings and their implications are presented in the first six chapters. Material of a more technical nature, including prior research, design and methodology, and tabular arrays of data, is presented in the appendices.

ACKNOWLEDGMENTS

The fieldwork for this project occurred over an eight-year period and the writing spanned an additional two years. Needless to say, a great many people helped me bring the project to fruition. I am especially indebted to Anthony Athos, Jay Lorsch, and Richard Walton for their initial guidance in the early stages of the research. Thanks are due also to Jay Norman and Frank Leonard for their assistance in the initial fieldwork. The decision to extend the project beyond the first set of studies was largely a result of the advice and support of E. Raymond Corey who was then director of research at the Harvard Business School. When I was long behind schedule, he urged me to "go back to the data" instead of bringing premature closure to the project. He also encouraged me to undertake a second set of studies and provided the financial as well as moral support to do so. Without his encouragement the project would not have taken its final form. Also instrumental in urging me to extend the project were Derek Abell and Pierre Goetchin and their colleagues at IMEDE in Lausanne. My closest colleague in extending the research was Colleen Kaftan. Without her assistance in both the analysis and fieldwork, I could not have completed the project. Her insights, support, and optimism kept me and the research going.

I also owe a large debt of gratitude to my colleague John Kotter for his help in the final comparative analysis. The shape this book has taken is very much a consequence of his suggestions, probing questions, and persistence.

Several colleagues read an earlier draft of the book in its entirety. I am particularly grateful to Linda Hill, Paul Lawrence, George Lombard, Michael Lombardo, Morgan McCall, Leonard Schlesinger, Jeffrey Sonnenfeld, and Richard Vancil for their detailed and helpful suggestions.

A number of other colleagues helped with criticisms, suggestions, and comments. I would like to thank especially, Eugene Andrews, Michael Arthur, Louis Barnes, James Baughman, Jon Bentz, Thomas Bonoma, Richard Boyatzis, Eliza Collins, Stuart Friedman, Donald Hambrick, Robert Kaplan, Meryl Louis, Samuel Rabinowitz, Donald Schön, Peter Smith, Rosemary Stewart, Renato Tagiuri, and Arthur Turner.

Finally, there are three people whose counsel had a particular impact on this book. Robert Eccles, Russell Eisenstadt, and Jay Lorsch read and commented on two drafts in detail. Although I have not acted on all of their suggestions, the finished product has benefited substantially from their advice and criticisms.

These acknowledgments would not be complete without also thanking several people who provided material support for the research. I am especially grateful to Dean John McArthur of the Harvard Business School for providing me with release time to complete the project, and to Richard Rosenbloom, who was director of research at the outset of the study, for funding the project as well as for his useful insights and criticism on early working papers. I am also grateful to Rose Giacobbe, Susan Greismer, and Margaret Nayduch who ensured that three drafts and endless revisions were processed competently and quickly and to Michael Stephenson for his assistance in the literature reviews.

For reasons of confidentiality I cannot thank by name the fourteen companies and seventeen managers and their staffs who participated in the research. Their openness and generosity of time provided the reality from which this book was wrought. Finally, I want to thank my wife Marilyn and my children Jana and Jorde for enduring the long life of the project with cheerfulness and understanding.

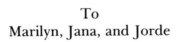

To
Marilyn, Jana, and Jorde

The
Dynamics
of Taking
Charge

1

INTRODUCTION

The longer you're in the new job, the more you develop a personal sense of comfort. You go from a period when you're on the edge of your seat all the time—it feels like you have no knowledge base whatsoever about anything. You have to learn the product, the people, the situation, and the problems. It takes a period of time before you develop a comfortable feeling. It just plain takes awhile. You go through an early period of first trying like hell to learn about the organization. You're faced with a set of problems that are foreign to you. You have to learn about the people and their capabilities awfully fast and that's the trickiest thing to do. At first you're afraid to do anything for fear of upsetting the apple cart. The problem is you have to keep the business *running* while you *learn* about it.

These remarks are excerpted from an interview with a newly appointed division general manager who was eighteen months into his new assignment. I chose his comments to begin this book because they capture the flavor of the work: the challenge, uncertainty, and excitement that many managers feel when they take charge of a new assignment. From the discomfort implicit in this manager's comments one might guess that he was a relatively young manager being tested for the first time. In fact, he was a seasoned manager who had spent over twenty years in executive assignments in sales, marketing, and manufacturing, both in consumer and industrial products.

At the time of the interview, this manager was far more

comfortable than he had been six months earlier; more pieces had fallen into place and some of the changes he had made during his first six months had worked. He nonetheless felt that there was a great deal more to do before he had the $175 million division functioning the way he wanted. He had reorganized the division from a product to a functional structure after his first twelve months and was now awaiting corporate approval for further changes. It would, in fact, take another ten months for these changes to be implemented and shaken down, though when he started he did not know that. In another interview with me some eighteen months later he said he finally had things running the way he wanted. By then, he had brought about one of the most successful division turnarounds in his corporation's history.

This book is about the process of taking charge: how managers learn about their new assignments, act on that learning, and do the organizational and interpersonal work necessary to take charge of their organizations. It also concerns the factors—situational and personal—that influence how managers take charge, and tells us why some managers succeed in taking charge while others do not.

Dramatic examples of management successions capture the public's attention and often make headlines in the business and popular press. These often involve colorful figures in large corporations, often companies in trouble. Yet management succession is fairly commonplace in organizational life; managers take charge of new assignments every day at every level. A recent study of general managers conducted by John Kotter showed that the managers in his sample (average age forty-seven) had taken charge of new management jobs anywhere from 3 to 9 times during their careers, the average being between 5 and 6.[1]

Despite its common occurrence, the process of taking charge is perhaps one of the least understood activities in management. The topic has not been explicitly or systematically studied by either management theorists or organizational psychologists. Although a great deal of research has been done on the broader topic of management succession,[2] very little has focused on the activities and problems faced by the new manager *after* he begins a new job and actually takes charge. It is this gap in the succession process—what managers do to take charge—that this book addresses.

The Managers in the Study

This book is based on research consisting of three sets of field studies involving seventeen management successions of general managers and functional managers in organizations in the United States and Europe. The sample was chosen to get a range of industries, jobs, management levels, and size of revenue responsibility. Revenues of the new managers' units ranged from $1.2 million to $3 billion, with most between $100 million and $800 million. Over two-thirds of the participants were general managers while the rest were upper-level functional executives. Their industries ranged from computers to consumer products and from injection molding to machine tools. One participant was in the public sector.

The sample included successions in which the new manager had failed as well as those in which he had succeeded as well as successions that were turnarounds and those which were not. Table 1-1 summarizes the managers studied, their jobs, revenue responsibilities, industries, and locations. The first set of cases was studied longitudinally over three years as these new managers actually went about the process of taking charge of their new assignments. This study was designed to yield data points at the 3-, 6-, 12-, 15-, 18-, 24-, 27-, 30-, 36-, and 42-month periods. The second set of cases was studied retrospectively, covering the first three years of the new manager's tenure. The third set was targeted to examine the first six months, the 12- to 24-month period and the 6- to 36-month period (see Appendix A for a detailed description of the research design and methods).

Table 1-1
Summary Description of Managers Studied

Unit's Business	Unit Revenues* ($)	Manager's Job	Predecessor as Superior	Turnaround Situation	Industry-Specific Experience	Insider (I) or Outsider (O) to Organization	Location	Succession Success (S) or Failure (F)**	Case Number
Longitudinal Case Studies									
Industrial and office products division	260 million	Division president	yes	no	yes	I	U.S.	S	(1)
Machine-tool division	175 million	Division president	no	yes	no	O	U.S.	S	(2)
Consumer products division	70 million	Division president	no	yes	no	O	U.S.	S	(3)
Construction-products division	55 million	Division president	yes	no	no	O	U.S.	S	(4)
Historical Case Studies (Retrospective)									
Cable television subsidiary	1.2 million	General manager	no	no	no	O	U.S.	F	(5)
Wholesale food distributor	21 million	Vice president sales and marketing	no	yes	no	O	U.S.	F	(10)
District sales organization (communications)	30 million	District manager	no	no	yes	I	U.S.	S	(11)

(continued)

4

Table 1-1
Summary Description of Managers Studied
(continued)

									Case Number
Beverage manufacturer	90 million	Managing director	no	yes	no	O	Netherlands	S	(6)
Plastic and metal products	100 million	Managing director	yes	no	yes	I	U.K.	F	(7)
Beverage manufacturer	110 million	Marketing and sales director	yes	no	no	O	Italy	F	(12)
Synthetic fibers	200 million	Director manufacturing	yes	yes	yes	I	U.K.	S	(13)
Computer and technical products	780 million	General manager and vice president	no	no	yes	I	Switzerland	S	(8)
Industrial and consumer products	3 billion	Chief executive	no	yes	yes	I	U.K.	S	(9)
Public education	Not available	Functional manager	no	yes	yes	I	U.S.	S	(14)
Supplementary Case Studies (Targeted)									
Plastic components	80 million	General manager	no	no	yes	O	U.S.	S	(15)
Heavy equipment	500 million	General manager	no	no	no	O	U.S.	S	(16)
Computer products	650 million	Subsidiary president	no	no	no	O	U.S.	S	(17)

*Unit revenues expressed in 1982 U.S. dollars.

**A succession was considered a failure if the new manager was fired within the first 36 months because of his inability to meet top management's expectations of performance.

A Definition of Taking Charge

Before describing what this book will cover, I want to be explicit about what I mean by "taking charge." By taking charge, I do not mean just orienting oneself to a new assignment. Taking charge, as I use the term, refers to the process by which a manager establishes mastery and influence in a new assignment. By mastery, I mean acquiring a grounded understanding of the organization, its tasks, people, environment, and problems. By influence, I mean having an impact on the organization, its structure, practices, and performance. The process begins when a manager starts a new assignment and ends when he or she has mastered it in sufficient depth to be managing the organization as efficiently as the resources, constraints, and the manager's own ability allow. By this definition, the manager quoted at the beginning had not yet fully taken charge, despite the fact that he was eighteen months into his assignment at the time of the interview.

Summary of the Findings

Defined in these terms, taking charge is a process which involves a great many activities. The managers in the study took charge in very different ways depending on their management styles, skills, prior experience, and, obviously, the situations they faced. Despite these differences, several patterns stood out.

STAGES OF LEARNING AND ACTION

The first is that the taking-charge process can be characterized as occurring in a series of predictable stages of learning and action. In successful transitions, managers progressed through these stages as they gained greater knowledge and mastery of their assignments. These stages are: (1) Taking Hold—a period of orientational and evaluative learning and corrective action;

(2) Immersion—a period of relatively little change but more reflective and penetrating learning; (3) Reshaping—a period of major change during which the new manager acts on the deeper understanding he gained in the preceding stage; (4) Consolidation—a period in which earlier changes are consolidated; and (5) Refinement—a period of fine-tuning and relatively little major additional learning. By the final stage, the new manager has acquired an in-depth understanding of the organization and its situation and has had an impact on it. In the U.S. cases it took from two and a half to three years for managers to progress through these stages.

The organizational changes managers made as they worked through these stages characteristically occurred in three waves: the first wave occurs during the Taking-Hold stage, the second, and typically largest, during the Reshaping stage, and the last and smallest during the Consolidation stage. These stage and wave patterns are found in successful transitions regardless of the kind of succession (insider versus outsider; turnaround versus nonturnaround), the industry of the organization involved, or the manager's prior functional background.

EFFECTS OF BACKGROUND AND SITUATION

Background and situational factors also influence a manager's progression through the stages and the problems he is likely to encounter. The most prominent of these factors are a manager's prior functional and industry-specific experience. Particularly in the early stages, a manager's prior experience *profoundly* influences the manager's actions and what he tends to focus on, as well as the kinds of problems he is likely to face. This pattern is so pervasive in the cases studied that it has important implications for managers taking charge as well as for their superiors in anticipating and action-planning potential problems. Differences also exist in the problems faced by managers taking charge of turnarounds versus nonturnarounds and in the amount and nature of change they implement during the five stages.

The two most prevalent causes of failure to take charge are lack of prior experience relevant to the new assignment and poor working relationships with key people. Successful managers were more effective at the interpersonal work of developing mutual expectations, trust, and influence with both subordinates and superiors.

Cross-case comparisons also show that the successful managers were more effective at accomplishing three sets of organizational tasks: (1) assessing the organization and diagnosing its problems; (2) building a management team focused on a set of shared expectations; and (3) bringing about timely changes that address organizational problems.

In contrast, managers who failed approached these organizational tasks in a more solitary fashion, leading to what I describe as the "Lone Ranger Syndrome." Compared to the successful managers, they involved others—particularly superiors and subordinates—to a much lesser degree in the work of assessing and diagnosing organization problems. As a result, their diagnoses of situations tended to be much more narrowly focused and incomplete. They also used such team-focused devices as management group meetings and problem-focused task forces significantly less often than the successful managers. Finally, they made changes that were perceived as inappropriate or ineffective, either because the changes were based on partial or incorrect diagnoses of problems, or because the changes were badly implemented by a management group that did not support them.

Organization of the Book

The activities and factors that make a difference in how managers take charge are the subject of this book. Chapter 2 looks at the stages of learning and action and the issues and tasks that characterize these stages. Personal, background, situational, and interpersonal factors and their effects on the process are examined in detail in chapter 3. Chapters 4 and 5 treat at a more operational level the organizational and interpersonal work required to take charge effectively, and the patterns found in successful transitions. Finally, chapter 6 draws a number of operational and policy implications for new managers taking charge and for senior executives and corporate staff personnel involved in succession planning and transition management. The overall purpose of the book is to help new managers be more effective in this important, multifaceted transition and to provide senior executives and corporate staffs responsible for succession decisions with concepts for better managing these transitions.

Notes

1. See John P. Kotter, *The General Managers* (New York: Free Press, 1982).
2. Please see Appendix B for a more detailed review of studies relevant to the process of taking charge.

2

STAGES OF TAKING CHARGE

The learning and action that managers engage in to take charge can vary substantially, as do the issues they face. Consider, for example, the following brief summaries of two successful cases. In one, the manager had been promoted from within, while in the other, he had come from outside the industry.

Tom Kane took charge of a $260 million industrial- and office-products division with a mandate from corporate headquarters to improve margins, increase share of market, and grow the division to $400 million within three to five years. Before assuming the division's presidency, Kane had been a group officer in another part of the parent corporation but previously had spent twenty-five years in the division and knew its industry, products, and people well. As a result of his experience, Kane had a fairly specific plan of what changes he wanted to make once he took charge, and he had discussed them with corporate staff in some detail before beginning the assignment. Kane spent his first three months checking his prior assumptions about people, problems, and the organization. Having confirmed his assessments, Tom restructured the division from a functional to a geographic organization during his third month. This major reorganization involved a half dozen executive changes.

The results of the reorganization were almost immediate in terms of improved margins and coordination between manufacturing and sales. Kane did not anticipate the need to make any further changes and immersed himself in the process of making the changes work. After three or four months, however, Kane and his top management group became increasingly aware of sales and distribution problems in the United States and Canada that had not been evident under the earlier functional structure. As Tom probed the causes of the problems he also became aware of the limitations of several of the senior executives who were managing the division's sizable domestic operations. Though they had been superior managers in the former functional structure, they seemed not to have the breadth or general management skills necessary to manage within the new structure. This raised questions about whether he had the right people in place to grow the division to $400 million.

Kane worked on both sets of issues for nearly eleven months before he felt he understood them well enough to develop an action plan. As a result of his effort, Tom implemented a major reassignment of his top management group (involving eleven related personnel actions) in his sixteenth month and then restructured the division's domestic sales and marketing organization in his seventeenth month. The following six months were largely devoted to "shaking down" the new domestic sales organization, consolidating the changes he had made, and getting the "tigers" he now had as general managers working with one another. After twenty-seven months on the job, Tom saw his efforts pay off: the division had its best first quarter ever. By his thirty-first month, Tom felt he had finally mastered the situation. The changes he had made during his first two years were paying off: share of market was increasing rapidly and so were margins. Kane finally felt he had the structure and management group in place to grow the division's revenues to $400 million and he now turned his attention to divesting a product group which no longer fit in with the growth objectives of the division.

When Chet Ferguson took charge of the $175 million machine-tool division, his mandate was threefold: to stop the division's enormous losses; to create an organization that would be viable for the long run; and to develop at least two candidates to succeed him as president within five years. Ferguson had no previous experience in the machine-tool industry but had more than twenty years' experience in sales and manufacturing management, most recently as executive vice president for both functions in a $250 million precision parts division.

Unlike Kane, Ferguson had little first-hand knowledge of the division's business and no prior assessment or diagnosis of its problems. So he spent most of his first five months learning about the division, its personnel, and problems. During this period, he reported being overwhelmed at times by the amount of learning needed to orient himself, let alone assess and diagnose the situation.

During this period, Ferguson also worked at assessing his managers and their capabilities, but his major efforts focused on improving production planning by instituting and running weekly production meetings and implementing a number of improvements in planning and control systems, areas in which he had a great deal of expertise.

His initial five-month period of orientation and evaluation culminated with the decision to transfer the marketing and engineering staffs of the largest product group to the division's central functional staffs. Ferguson made these changes in order to get better "visibility" into the product group's problems as well as to get more divisional control over it since the product group was the source of the division's biggest losses. The results of these structural changes were quickly evident in better pricing decisions and improved delivery schedules.

During the next seven months, Ferguson made virtually no further changes. Instead, he continued to work at developing strength in his management group and improving the division's management practices. The success of the changes he had made in his fifth month, however, led him to question whether the division's structure should be changed from a relatively decentralized product organization to a functional one. He struggled with this question for nearly six months, engaged a consulting firm to study the problem, and finally concluded that a change to a functional structure would improve both coordination and control.

Ferguson implemented the reorganization during his twelfth through fourteenth months—a major reorganization comparable to the one Kane, an industry insider, had implemented after only three months. Unlike Kane, however, it took Ferguson more than ten months to consolidate the changes because of unanticipated problems and the need to transfer and hire people for several new positions. By Ferguson's twenty-sixth month, the reorganization was fully shaken down and the division had finished a profitable year. Ferguson and his top management group then spent the next six months developing a new strategic plan. Ferguson now felt that he had finally "put the road map in place." No major changes were made during the next ten months, and the division was among the most profitable in the corporation. Ferguson was now actively identifying potential successors.

Learning and Action Stages

Although these cases differ in many respects, Ferguson and Kane and the other managers studied went through a similar process of learning and action-taking.

Two patterns stand out from the data when the taking-charge process is examined over time. The first is that taking charge can be a long process at upper and middle levels of management: from two to two and a half years for senior-level U.S. managers and even longer for some European and U.K. senior-level managers. Second, as the two cases just cited illustrate, is that the taking-charge process is not one of steadily increasing learning or action. Rather it consists of a series of stages in which the new manager's emphasis alternates between learning and action in what appears to be a sequentially predictable fashion.

I use "learning" and "action" in their broadest meanings. By learning, I mean the orientation work of figuring out a new assignment or situation as well as the assessment and diagnostic work of determining how to improve the organization's performance. By action, I mean both organizational and personnel changes that the new manager makes to influence the organization's performance; these range from corrective changes that deal with only certain aspects of the organization to those that are sufficiently profound to reshape an organization.

Before discussing these stages in detail, I shall first describe them broadly. In the first stage, *Taking Hold,* which typically lasts from three to six months, the new manager takes hold of the assignment. There is a great deal of learning and action. The learning is mainly orientational and evaluative, and the new manager focuses principally on problems that become apparent to him based on his past experience and what he learns about the situation during his first three to five months. The changes he makes, even if they are major, tend to be corrective; they deal with problems he is able to identify and diagnose early in his succession. By the end of this Taking-Hold period, he understands the situation fairly well and has acted on those problems he understands.

In the next stage, *Immersion,* the manager immerses himself in running the organization in a more informed fashion. During this time, which typically lasts from four to eleven months, the manager makes very few changes. It is, however, a period that is potentially very important for learning that is deeper than the orientational and evaluative learning of the first stage. When the new manager develops either a more detailed concept of how further to improve performance or, in many cases, a significant reconceptualization of how the organization's structure and practices should be altered, the Immersion stage is over.

The concept that develops from the Immersion stage provides the impetus for the next stage, *Reshaping,* which is typically a period of intense change usually lasting from three to six months. During this time, the new manager acts on the learning of the previous stage. Most of the major structural changes of the first three years in the cases I studied were made during this stage.

The taking-charge process then continues into a period of *Consolidation,* in which the new manager and his group attempt to consolidate the changes made in the Reshaping stage. Consolidation typically lasts three to nine months. The learning early in this stage tends to be evaluative, focusing mainly on the results of the major changes made in the earlier period. By the middle of this stage, the manager begins to make a number of corrective changes aimed at consolidating the directions implemented during the Reshaping stage.

The completion of the taking-charge process is marked by a transition into a *Refinement* stage, in which most of the manager's additional learning is a consequence of dealing with the day-to-day problems of running the business rather than his newness to the job or the need to work on major underlying problems. In the cases studied, no significant organizational changes were made by the new managers thereafter, except in one case where an acquisition was made at the forty-month period. Otherwise, the period from twenty-seven to forty-two months involved relatively minor organizational change.

The Three-Wave Phenomenon

The stage pattern is most visible in the timing and magnitude of the changes new managers make during their first three years on the job. When one plots organizational actions, such as personnel and structural changes, over time, the changes tend to cluster in three waves of action corresponding to the stages just described. These three waves can be seen quite clearly in Figure 2-1 which presents a plotting of the average number of organizational changes made each quarter for the first thirty-six months of taking charge. The organizational change measure shown is a composite of both structural and personnel changes made per quarter, but the same three-wave pattern is found when the measure is disaggregated by either structural or personnel changes.[1]

I have called this pattern the "three-wave" phenomenon because it shows up consistently, regardless of how the activity data are disaggregated. Figure 2-2 breaks out the sample for different types of successions, including turnarounds, nonturnarounds, insider successions, and outsider successions.[2] Again the same pattern is found.

Figure 2-1
Average Number of Organizational Changes per Three-Month Period
Following Succession*

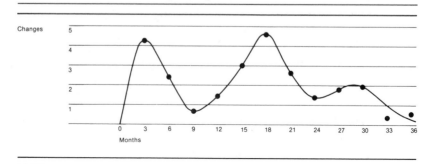

*Averages based on change data from the successful cases in the longitudinal and historical studies.

Figure 2-2
Average Number of Organizational Changes per Six-Month Period
Following Succession, Categorized*

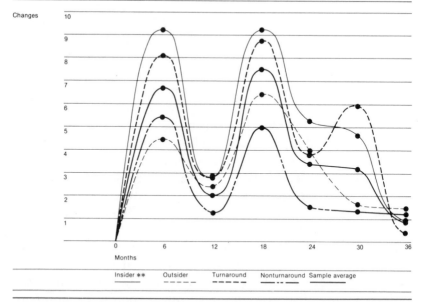

*Averages based on change data from the successful cases in the longitudinal and historical studies.
**Insider successions are those in which the new manager had five or more years' experience in the new organization's industry.

The three-wave pattern also characterizes successions in which the new managers took over smoothly running and effective organizations, where one would expect relatively little need for change or where whatever change was necessary might be either consolidated in one wave or spread out more evenly over time. Finally the three-wave pattern shows up on a case-by-case basis with relatively few exceptions (the exceptions were cases in which only the first two major clusters of activity appeared).

Case-by-case, the three waves generally peaked at between 3 and 6 months, 15 and 20 months and 27 and 30 months. Typically, the second wave was the largest and the third wave was, without exception, the smallest (see Appendix C for examples of plottings of this data on an individual basis).

What accounts for this pervasive pattern? Why were the major changes made by the new managers invariably clustered in three waves of action? One can speculate that it takes time to plan and implement major changes under any circumstances, let alone while a manager is also taking charge, and therefore peak-change periods will always be separated. Or, perhaps managers intuitively "pile up" the changes they want to make and implement them all at once to minimize organizational disruption. Neither of these explanations, however, accounts for why there are typically three waves of change, not one, with the second wave usually the largest, and the third wave always the smallest; nor do they explain why half the managers in the longitudinal studies believed that their *first* wave of action would take care of all of the major changes required and did not discern the need for further major change until later in the study.

I also considered that these change patterns might in some way be related to annual budgeting and planning cycles. This might have been a viable explanation if all seventeen managers had taken charge of their assignments on January first or on the first day of their firm's fiscal year. Yet the successions began in almost every month of the year; only one manager began his assignment effective the beginning of his firm's reporting year. Thus budget and reporting cycles are also an inadequate explanation for this periodicity.

Perhaps the three-wave phenomenon was an artifact of the research design itself, i.e., the very process of studying new managers on a scheduled basis (at the 3-, 6-, 12-, 18-, 30-, etc.-month periods) could have influenced the timing and magnitude of the changes they made. One could argue that the new managers might have used the periodic interviews as catalysts for introspection and as occasions for organizing their thoughts, which in turn mobilized them to take actions in patterns that reflected the periodicity. The result would be a more orderly and clustered pattern of action than normal. The problem is, however, that although this explanation might apply to the longitudinal cases, in which I studied the new managers as they actually went about taking charge, it would not apply to the historical cases, which were studied retrospectively. In those ten cases the data were gathered after the fact and there was no possibility of a researcher effect. Yet the same three-wave clustering was found in these cases as well, as shown in Figures 2-1 and 2-2.

Although I could speculate further, my interview and observational data suggest that the three-wave pattern is closely related to the way managers learn about their new situations and how they then act on that learning. The experience of following the longitudinal cases as they actually unfolded and of listening to managers and their key subordinates describe what they were doing as the new managers took charge leads me to believe that the three waves are natural consequences of how new managers learn and act as they try to master a new situation.

Managers, as Argyris and Schön have demonstrated, learn from the results of their actions,[3] but the results of changes made in complex organizations take time to play themselves out. Thus, it takes time for a manager to learn from the results of the changes he makes as he takes charge. Moreover, as I will show later, changes reconfigure the situation, opening up new opportunities for further learning and diagnosis at least until the manager has largely mastered the situation. Finally, the more familiar a manager becomes with a situation, the fewer opportunities he has for significant incremental learning. This is one explanation for why the wave pattern diminishes after twenty-seven to thirty months.

Seen in these learning and action terms, the wave pattern corresponds to the stages I have described, as Figure 2-3 illustrates. The first stage, Taking Hold, coincides with the first wave of change because it is a period in which the new manager is not only learning about the situation but applying what he knows from past experience to act on that learning when he makes corrective changes.

Because the consequences of changes take time to appear, the second stage, Immersion, corresponds to the trough between the first and second wave. This trough also occurs because the new manager, having acted on what he felt needed to be changed, now immerses himself in managing the organization more knowledgeably. The relatively change-free Immersion period further provides an opportunity for deeper and more reflective learning than was possible in the first stage, because the manager is now better informed and able to see underlying patterns.[4]

It is not surprising, then, that the deeper understanding that emerges from the Immersion stage typically yields a new conceptualization of the situation. This becomes the basis of the major changes made in the Reshaping stage, which coincides with the second and typically largest wave of change.

Finally, the Consolidation stage reflects both the manager's assessment of changes made in the Reshaping stage and the actions he takes to correct and consolidate them. This stage corresponds to the small third wave and the trough before it.*

Before proceeding to a more detailed description of the stages, I wish again to stress that the length of time individual managers spent in each of these stages varied greatly. The

---

*It could be argued that the Consolidation stage comprises two parts. The first would be an assessment period corresponding to the trough between the second and third waves in which the new manager and his group review, analyze, and learn from the actions of the Reshaping stage. The second part of Consolidation could be conceptualized as a period in which consolidating and corrective changes are made based on the assessment that preceded it. This second part would correspond to the third wave.

Figure 2-3
Organizational Change Activity and Corresponding Stages
of Learning and Action

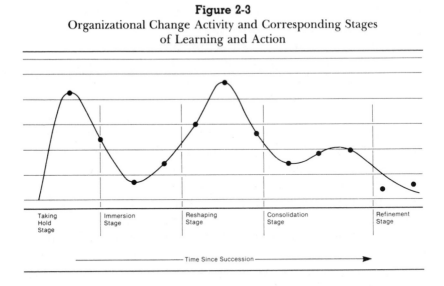

| Taking Hold Stage | Immersion Stage | Reshaping Stage | Consolidation Stage | Refinement Stage |

Time Since Succession ⟶

stages are *not* defined by elapsed time; they are defined by learning and action issues.

Taking Hold

I have called the first stage Taking Hold because it was during this initial stage, typically lasting from three to six months, that the new managers attempted to grasp the nature of their new situations, understand what tasks and problems needed to be dealt with, and assess their organization's capabilities. In simplest terms, the new managers tried to learn as much as they could about their new assignments and act on those problems they believed needed tackling.

The learning that occurs during this stage is principally *orientational* and *evaluative* and results in the new manager's developing a cognitive map of his situation by the middle to the end of the period. By "cognitive map" I mean a mental model or picture of the organization, its key actors, and the important factors that affect its functioning and performance.[5] Managers promoted from within obviously begin with a better cognitive map, and their learning is acquired from the perspective of being the person in charge. For an outsider, especially one who comes from outside the organization's industry, developing a cognitive map of the situation requires a great deal of learning. If the new assignment is a major promotion or change, the new manager may at times feel overwhelmed.

In those cases where the new manager was an outsider to the organization, the orientational learning meant acquiring an understanding of the business, products, competition, cost structure, and so forth, as well as of how the organization itself worked. The orientational learning was especially demanding if the new manager came from another industry. For example, the new president of a computer products subsidiary, an industry outsider, described the task as being so large that "even locking myself up for four days to review strategic, financial, marketing, and industry reports barely made a dent in it." Early in this stage he also said he needed several hours just to go through the morning mail, not only because the issues were new to him but because the computer industry's technical jargon and nomenclature were still foreign to him. Another manager in a similar situation voiced his exasperation by simply saying "there aren't enough hours in the day."

If the new manager had been promoted from within or was not an industry outsider, the orientational learning was usually less overwhelming and typically focused on unfamiliar aspects of the business. The new CEO of a $3 billion group who had spent his entire career in the operations end of the business began by systematically studying all of the group's strategy documents, plans, and budgets. Then he shifted to the group's finances, an area he had not previously worked in but which he felt was critical since the group managed its own financing. As he put it, "You've got to keep the bankers away from your door or it's no use talking about strategy." With this as background he proceeded to focus intensely on the group's strategic and planning functions. All of these aspects of the organization, with which he had no in-depth exposure, were, he felt, essential for him to master his new job as CEO.

The learning that occurs during the Taking-Hold stage is also *evaluative*. Much effort was devoted to assessing key subordinates, where the problems lay, and very important, one's priorities. This evaluative learning varied by situation, and in five of the turnarounds it also had a charged urgency: "how to stop the bleeding."

For insiders already familiar with their organizations, both the evaluative and orientational learning of the Taking-Hold period typically did not involve as much "front-end" work as it did for outsiders. More often, the new manager consciously or tacitly tested his assumptions about the organization and its problems.

For one new division president, described at the beginning of the chapter, who had over twenty-five years in his organization, evaluative learning meant testing both his assumptions about key people and his prior assessment of the division's problems. This occupied a large portion of his first three months and resulted in a number of conclusions, including the belief that one of his senior vice presidents (SVP) was "over his head." The assessment was based on a number of meetings with the SVP and his subordinates, the man's previous five-year plan, complaints about "cliques" in his area, problems with other functions, and the man's insensitive treatment of two of the firm's major overseas distributors. The new president found the insensitive treatment particularly troublesome because it indicated he could not trust the man's judgment. Such testing of prior assumptions characterized most of the insider successions and typically took a variety of forms.

The Taking-Hold stage also involves a great deal of action, which typically peaked between three and six months. Nearly a third of all the structural and personnel changes made during the first three years occurred during the first six-month period (the percentage change data are presented in Appendix C, Figure C-3). Although the stages do *not* neatly portion themselves out into six-month periods case-by-case, this figure does give some indication of how much action took place in this period, since Taking Hold lasted only from three to six months in most of the cases.

Organizational changes made during this stage tend to be *corrective:* they address problems that either become apparent to the new manager as he develops his cognitive map or were already apparent to him before he took charge. To put it bluntly, the new manager "fixes" those problems he knows how to fix based on his past experience and what he has learned about the new situation.

The nature of these corrective actions obviously varies. In turnarounds they often involved immediate changes to deal with urgent problems, such as the introduction of a cost system, a reduction in the product line, or a change in reporting relationships. The new manager may take these actions even if he has not yet had the time to do a strategic analysis or even develop an action agenda. The problem may be so urgent and obvious to the new manager that he knows, based on his past experience, that it must be acted on. In one turnaround, a new general manager of a $70 million consumer-products division knew by the end of the second week that the division needed a better cost system in manufacturing; by the end of the first month he realized that the product line had to be reduced if losses were to be stemmed. Although it took nearly five months before he had developed a complete strategy for turning the division around, he understood that, based on his past experience, both a cost system and a reduction in the product line were needed immediately.

The corrective actions of the Taking-Hold period do not always involve immediate, short-term interventions. The CEO of the $3 billion group described earlier, who was also involved in a turnaround, approached this stage quite differently. Having been promoted from within and having himself previously turned around the manufacturing part of the business, his initial actions were not significant short-term corrections but were focused on product strategy and on establishing product policy committees and new product project teams. Although his actions did not have the same "fix-it" quality of those taken in the general manager's turnaround, they were nonetheless corrective. They dealt with areas that the new CEO saw as lacking but critical to his group's success.

Not only does the nature of the corrective actions taken in this stage vary, depending on the situation, but so does the magnitude, depending on the new manager's prior knowledge and his perception of the need for change. Kane, the division president with twenty-five years' prior experience described earlier, implemented a major reorganization of his division in his third month in office. In contrast, the division presidents who were outsiders to their division's industries, like Ferguson, did not implement comparable organizational changes until their second year in office, well beyond the Taking-Hold stage. The difference lies in the first president's greater knowledge of the division's operations and problems, and his conviction that the division needed to be restructured and that he knew how to do it.

Most of the examples discussed so far have concerned successions of division- or group-level general managers and have therefore involved changes in organization structure and product policy. In successions of upper-level functional managers and middle-level general managers, however, the corrective actions of the Taking-Hold stage tended to involve less dramatic changes and were focused more on systems and practices than on structure. Nonetheless, the same pattern of corrective actions was found.

In summary, the Taking-Hold period is one of intense learning during which the new manager develops a cognitive map of the new situation and takes corrective action on those problems he understands and knows how to address, be they as immediate as cutting the product line or as far-reaching as conducting a strategic business analysis. Whatever the case, this stage involves some action and typically a flurry of it by the middle to the end of the stage.

Immersion

Although managers typically experienced the learning of this stage as being much less demanding than that of the Taking-Hold stage, their interviews revealed that the Immersion stage was a *very* important period of deeper learning and diagnosis. In the U.S. cases, the period lasted from four to eleven months.

Unlike the Taking-Hold period, the Immersion stage involves relatively little organizational change activity (see Figure 2-3). Only 6 percent of the structural and 9 percent of the personnel changes were made during the second six months, which generally coincided with the onset of this stage (see Appendix C for a presentation of this data). This dramatic decrease in organizational change from the first six months occurred partly because the new manager had already taken action on those issues he understood in the Taking-Hold period.

The second stage is named "Immersion" because during this period the new managers immersed themselves not only in running their organizations in a more informed fashion but in a process of less hectic and finer-grained learning than had been previously possible. The successful managers acquired this finer-grained understanding for two reasons. First, they now knew enough about the situation to be able to see subtleties that had escaped them earlier. Second, they had been at the new job long enough to develop a sufficient experience base to see patterns that had not been evident earlier. In five cases, the new managers found that despite changes they had made in the Taking-Hold stage, some of the same problems persisted, although perhaps manifested differently. Conversely, in seven cases, the new managers found that *because* certain changes made earlier *did* work, new problems became visible. These problems were not apparent earlier because they had been masked by difficulties that the Taking-Hold actions had addressed. Moreover, some issues that new managers had only partially understood in their first three to six months became more concrete during the Immersion stage because their experience base had grown, or simply because they had struggled with them longer. This pattern was evident in seven of the successful cases.

To a great degree, the finer-grained and, in many cases, deeper and more reflective learning of the Immersion stage is possible because of the work done in the Taking-Hold stage. In one case, for instance, cost problems in manufacturing persisted after the new manager of a $55 million construction-products division had made several major changes during the Taking-Hold stage. These changes included reorganizing manufacturing by product lines (the division's two product lines were quite different) and implementing better control, scheduling, and cost systems. Although these changes had made a visible difference, costs were still too high. The new manager and his subordinates continued to struggle with this problem during the Immersion stage and, as their understanding of the situation deepened, they realized that many of the cost problems were rooted in the product's design, and ultimately in how the division's engineering group was structured. It took, however, six to eight months of exploration before this underlying cause became clear.

Even when the changes made in the Taking-Hold stage *did* work, the Immersion stage still yielded potential further learning. What occurred under these circumstances was that new problems began to emerge which were not visible to the new manager earlier because they were masked or over-shadowed by larger problems. For example, Kane, the division president who had implemented a major reorganization of his division in his third month, discovered a new set of problems during the Immersion period that neither he nor his management team had seen earlier. The reorganization he had implemented in the Taking-Hold stage had changed the $260 million division from a functional to a geographic structure, with a domestic-international split. This change significantly improved the division's responsiveness, productivity, and coordination among functions within the United States and abroad. As the original cross-functional problems began to diminish, however, a number of new problems concerning the U.S. sales force's organization and its channels of distribution became visible. These problems were not obvious during the Taking-Hold stage because they had been hidden by the more basic cross-functional problems existing under the old organization structure. When the reorganization alleviated these more basic problems, the sales force and channels problems were revealed. These problems did not magically stand up and announce themselves after the reorganization, of course. They surfaced in large part as a result of the better understanding that the new president and his group acquired as he continued to work at mastering the new assignment. This was a much more subtle, exploratory, and detailed kind of learning than had occurred during the Taking-Hold stage, despite the fact that the new president had over twenty-five years of experience in the division.

I do not believe that this process of immersion and exploration happens by choice or design, although I suspect that how deeply it goes is influenced by the manager's desire to master his assignment. The new manager has already acted on whatever problems were apparent in the Taking-Hold stage and he now naturally begins to look more closely at issues that were either below the surface or not so obvious earlier. This deeper and more concrete understanding develops even when the manager has made a detailed and thorough analysis of the situation in the Taking-Hold stage, because the fine-grained and more probing learning of the Immersion period is a natural outgrowth of the interactions, problems, and conflicts that the new manager has to deal with day-to-day. In the longitudinal studies, the learning gained in this stage resulted in the new managers' developing a much better and deeper understanding of the basic issues and underlying problems. This was especially true for managers who were new to the organization or business.

Interviews during this period often showed managers asking questions like: Is the basic structure right? Are our channels of distribution wrong? Why do we continue to have cost problems in manufacturing despite improvements in production and inventory control? Interviews also showed that during the Immersion stage the new manager questioned more sharply whether he had the right people in place. Typically, obvious competence problems had been treated in the Taking-Hold stage, but now the questions became more subtle. As will be discussed in chapter 4, the new manager began to know many key subordinates and their strengths and limitations better during the Immersion stage than had been possible in the Taking-Hold stage.

Similarly, if in the Taking-Hold stage the manager had developed some notions of changes that needed to be made but that he felt uncertain about implementing, he typically explored these questions further and in more depth during the Immersion stage, in his own mind and in discussions with others. I observed this type of exploration in over half the cases. Interviews during this period suggested that the new manager selectively attended to details and events that might clarify whether such changes would be useful and what problems he might expect in implementing them.

In all of the longitudinal cases, the Immersion period culminated with the new manager developing either a different concept of what needed to be done than he had at the end of the Taking-Hold stage, or a much more refined concept of how the organization could be made more effective. The analysis, probing, discussion—in some cases, agonizing—of the Immersion stage results in a better understanding of the more basic dynamics of the business, its people, and organization. The concept that emerges from this stage (whether new or refined) is not necessarily radical; however, in eight of the seventeen cases, the revised concept had implications for major changes in strategy or organization or both. In most cases the result was a sharper plan of action for improving the situation.

Even in cases of experienced insiders who began their successions with a sizable amount of understanding and insight into their organizations and business, the Immersion stage still led to a better, or at least a more detailed, concept of what needed to be done to improve the situation. For example, in the case of the division president cited earlier, the concept that emerged involved relatively detailed ideas of how the division's U.S. sales and marketing functions ought to be reorganized as well as a specific concept of how to reassign his top management team to make the new organization structure he had implemented earlier work. Despite his obvious competence and intimate knowledge of the business, he had simply needed, as he put it, the additional time and experience to figure out what was required to implement his new strategy and structure effectively.

In summary, the Immersion stage is a period of relatively

little change activity, but of important continued learning. The nature of this learning is less intense than in the Taking-Hold stage, but is more fine-grained, more diagnostic, subtle, and, in most cases, more probing in nature. As a result of this better understanding the manager's cognitive map becomes fuller and more detailed, and he revises his concept of what needs to be done to effect further improvements.

Reshaping

If the Immersion stage is characterized by relatively little change, the third stage, Reshaping, is the opposite. This is the period of the second major wave of action, which in most cases was the largest. Learning and diagnosis continues, but in a more diminished and routine fashion. I call this stage reshaping because the new manager's principal activities are now directed at reconfiguring one or more aspects of the organization to implement the concept developed during the Immersion stage. He reshapes the organization to deal with the underlying issues he explored during the earlier stage.

The Reshaping stage is similar to the Taking-Hold because it involves much organizational change. Over 32 percent of the management personnel changes and 30 percent of the structural changes were made during this six-month period. (Again, the stages being described did not neatly portion themselves into six-month periods; nonetheless, after thirteen to eighteen months most of the managers had reached Reshaping.)

By the time most managers reached this stage, they were eager to act on the added learning of the Immersion period. Indeed, the transition between the end of the Immersion stage and the beginning of the Reshaping stage usually involved a number of activities that paved the way for the changes of the Reshaping stage. In nine of the divisional and group successions, this entailed using internal task forces, outside consultants, or both. The end of the transition into the Reshaping stage was often characterized by the new manager (and often his key subordinates) becoming increasingly impatient to "get on with it." In one situation, the new president of a $650 million computer subsidiary had to fend off growing pressure from two of his vice presidents while he commissioned several internal task forces to focus on the areas of intended change. As he put it:

> The task force reports will take us to the point where there will be no surprises and a lot of added insights; the nice part of this is that everyone will know what needs to be done and they'll have ownership of the changes we need to make. If the obvious answer is wrong they'll flush it out. In the meantime, I have to convince these guys that the added time this is taking is worth it.

The changes made during the Reshaping stage often involve organizational processes and are not limited to structural changes alone. All of the general management successions had some element of structural change and, in most, major structural changes. In two of the division president successions, these changes entailed reorganizing from a product to a functional structure. In middle-level successions, however, the scope of the structural changes was significantly less dramatic than in the general manager or upper-level functional successions. This is not surprising, for the discretion to make structural or other major changes decreases as one goes down the hierarchy, as does the scope of the operation to be reshaped. More often, changes in functional successions involved procedures, practices, and in some cases, mission definitions. Whatever the situation, in all of the cases in which the new manager lasted in the job longer than eighteen months, there was some organizational change at this stage.

Reshaping is a very busy period for the manager and his direct reports, especially if major changes are being made. The case in which the U.S. marketing and sales units were being reorganized at the sixteen-month point required many meetings, with the managers being affected to work out details of relocations and positional changes and with each of the district sales forces to explain the changes. Key customers and distributors also had to be called on. Although the actual changes had been announced and published within a relatively short period, their implementation needed almost eight weeks of sustained activity by the new president, his new marketing VP, and his domestic sales manager. As would be expected, the learning and assessment of this stage is very intervention- and action-oriented, including searching for feedback on the sales reorganization's impact on key distributors, and its effects on orders.

The Reshaping stage ends when the new manager has implemented as much of the concept as circumstances allow, although interviews showed that several factors often prevented a complete implementation from occurring. The most prevalent of these was the unavailability of a person or persons needed to fill key positions.

Consolidation

In the fourth stage, Consolidation, comes the third and final wave of action in the taking-charge process. Much of the new manager's learning and action now focuses on consolidating and following through on changes made during the Reshaping stage. The learning, assessment, and diagnosis of this stage tend to be evaluative: the new manager and his key subordinates now assess the consequences of the changes made in the earlier wave of action and typically take corrective measures based on that learning.

The learning of this stage concerns two issues. The first is the time needed to implement fully and work out the details of many of the organizational or personnel changes initiated in the Reshaping period. Much Consolidation-stage learning focuses on identifying follow-through problems and ways of implementing further changes to deal with them.

In one division that had been reorganized from a product to a functional structure during the Reshaping stage, the new president had deferred integrating the manufacturing department of one of the former product groups into the divisional manufacturing function until after several other changes had been made. Now that the major part of the reorganization had been completed, he and his manufacturing vice president began to look more closely at the implementation required to integrate this product group and how best to organize it.

A second issue that arises during this stage is dealing with unanticipated problems that result from the changes made during the Reshaping stage. In four of the successful cases, for example, much of the nonroutine activity of the new managers during this stage was devoted to diagnosing these problems, learning about them, and correcting them.

Finally, during Consolidation, those aspects of the concept that could not be implemented in the Reshaping stage are dealt with as people or other resources become available. In another four cases this meant either waiting the necessary time to find and hire a person for an important position or transferring a manager already in the organization who could not be moved earlier.

In summary, the Consolidation stage involves considerably less organizational change than the Reshaping stage and considerably less incremental learning than the Taking-Hold and Immersion stages. In the U.S. cases, the Consolidation period varied from four to eight months in duration. This stage comes to an end when the new manager has consolidated and followed through all the changes initiated earlier.

Refinement

The final stage is Refinement, a period of relatively little organizational change. The manager had by this point "taken charge." In seven cases the new manager's actions and learning now focused either on refining operations or, in two other cases, looking for new opportunities in the marketplace or in new technology. In one of those situations this involved considering potential acquisitions, and in the other it meant possibly divesting part of the business.

Refinement is the end of the taking-charge process. The manager can now no longer be considered "new." The managers no longer felt new, nor were they seen or spoken of by their subordinates as being new. By now, managers had either established credibility and a power base or they had not; they also had had enough time to shape their situations and be judged by the results of their actions. If the manager was still uncomfortable with his situation, it was typically because of pressing business problems such as a recession or mounting interest rates, rather than his newness to the job.

Interviews during Refinement suggested this was a relatively calm period compared with the earlier stages. From this stage onward the manager's learning tended to be more slowly incremental and routine than it had been in the Taking-Hold, Immersion, Reshaping, and Consolidation stages. The calmness of this period can be destroyed by important developments in the economy, the marketplace, or technology. But whatever additional learning and action these events lead to, they cannot be attributed to the manager's newness. For better or worse, the manager has taken charge.

The Stages in Overview

From this description of these stages, it should be apparent that the nature and degree of both learning and action vary significantly as the new manager takes charge. Learning is orientational and evaluative in the Taking-Hold stage, but becomes more reflective, probing and finer-grained in the Immersion stage; it is distinctly intervention-oriented in the Reshaping period and largely evaluative in the Consolidation stage. Table 2-1 summarizes the kinds of learning and action that characterize each stage. What this Table describes is a *changing mix* of learning and action over the course of a management succession. In reality, all of the different kinds of learning and action can be found within every stage; however, the emphasis on each alters as the new manager proceeds to master the situation.

The persistence of the three-wave pattern raises some interesting questions that will be explored in later chapters. It sug-

Table 2-1
Learning and Action by Stage

	Taking Hold	Immersion	Reshaping	Consolidation	Refinement
Type of learning	Orientational, evaluative	Exploratory, reflective	Intervention-oriented	Evaluative	Routine
Learning outcomes	Cognitive map of new situation	Revised concept for change	Short-term assessments	Evaluative and corrective assessments	Incremental knowledge
Action outcomes	Corrective actions	Maintenance and/ or preparatory actions	Reshaping actions	Corrective actions	Maintenance actions

gests, for example, that taking charge, as I have defined it, does not occur overnight. A new manager needs time to have an impact on an organization, and changes take time to implement in an informed and intelligent fashion. Equally important, learning enough about a new situation to make changes that go beyond obvious problems requires not only the front-end work of the Taking-Hold stage but the deeper and finer-grained learning of the Immersion stage.

Factors Affecting Length of Stages

The duration of the stages varied from case to case. (Some sense of this variability can be seen by a comparison of the longitudinal cases shown in Appendix C.) One question the data raise is: What affects the duration of these stages on an individual-case basis? Generalizing from a study of seventeen successions is difficult, but it is possible, based on interview and observational data, to speculate about several factors that appear to have an effect on the duration of stages in individual successions. These include important externalities (such as a recession), the manager's own learning and management styles, the quality of his subordinates, and the norms of the larger organization or parent corporation.

It seems hardly accidental that the longest stage for each of the four presidents in the longitudinal studies coincided with the onset of recession in his industry (see Appendix C, Figure C-4). One might expect quite the opposite—that such a major external crisis would have the effect of hastening the process, accelerating the new manager's learning and the speed to act on those organizational changes he felt were necessary to improve performance. In each case, however, the exigencies of the recession provided a number of immediate problems to be dealt with: planning layoffs, reducing inventories and cutting costs, and managing cash (and relations with corporate headquarters) more carefully. These were very real problems that detracted from the principal learning and action activities of the stage in question, whether the reflective and preparatory work of the Immersion period or the less critical follow-up work of the Consolidation stage.

Despite the apparent (and conveniently "chartable") effects of the recession on the length of certain stages in the longitudinal cases, interviews and observations suggest that the manager himself—how he learns and his management style—is likely to have a far more profound effect on how long it takes him to work through individual stages than do dramatic externalities.

I do not think it is a coincidence that managers who were described by subordinates as having strong, hands-on, intervening management styles typically had long Immersion periods before getting to their second waves of actions. I suspect they became so captured by the details that it took them longer to do the reflective probing necessary to perform the deeper diagnostic work needed to reconceptualize the situation.

Similarly, the interviews in the retrospective studies also suggest that the norms and culture of the larger organization or parent can influence the length of certain stages, particularly Immersion. In two successions, the new managers made a point of explaining that the main reason they took so much time before making major organizational or policy changes in their second waves of action was that it was the company's style not to make significant changes without first exploring all of the possibilities and touching all bases. It is not surprising then that, although both of these successions had relatively normal

Taking-Hold periods (of about six months each), they also had the longest Immersion periods of all of the successions studied.

Two other factors can potentially affect the time a new manager takes to progress through these stages. One is the quality of the subordinates in place when the new manager arrives. If they lack ability or background, this cannot help but extend the time needed to complete the process of taking charge. If the new manager concludes that key subordinates are sufficiently hopeless to be terminated, he must then find replacements for them and this takes time, even when they are not searched for on the open market and are transferred from other parts of the parent organization. If the manager decides to work with them to improve their performance, this also takes time and will inevitably extend the length of the early stages.

Finally, external constraints in the form of corporate approvals for changes in systems, procedures, personnel, and structure also add time to the process, most typically in the Taking-Hold and Immersion stages.

Surprisingly, there are several factors that, based on the data, *do not* seem to affect the length of the stages. I expected that turnarounds might have led to shorter Taking-Hold stages or longer Immersion periods. There is, however, no evidence in the successions I studied that suggests that turnarounds differ from the others in the amount of time spent in any of the stages. Similarly, managers promoted from within did not have shorter stages than those who were brought in from the outside, although they did differ in other respects that will be described in the next chapter.

Do Managers Make Changes for the Sake of Change?

A final question which these stages raise is whether there is a tendency for new managers to make changes simply for the sake of change or because they believe that to get ahead they must make changes? The persistence of the three-wave phenomenon, even in successions in successful organizations, demands this question be asked or at least addressed. My own belief, based on my observations in tracking these successions, is that managers do not make these changes for the sake of change or to promote their own careers.

Although surely a way of leaving one's imprint on an organization is to change it, I think there is a much simpler explanation of why new managers made changes. As the next chapter will show, the actions a new manager took and the areas in which he involved himself, especially during the Taking-Hold stage, were very much influenced by his previous experience, and to some degree by certain stylistic preferences. I think that the change phenomenon described in this chapter occurred because new managers brought insights, preferences, and strengths to their assignments different from those of their predecessors; therefore, they focused on different aspects of the situation. Even in organizations with "thick" cultures, a new manager brings to the assignment a different mix of experience and managerial preferences than his predecessor. Indeed, one of the advantages of a change in management (if it is not done too frequently) is that a different set of eyes and ideas are brought to a situation. If the new manager is at all different from his predecessor and is at all performance-oriented, he is likely to see problems or patterns which his predecessor did not. I think this is especially true in general management successions where there is usually a larger range of issues to be addressed than in functional cases.

Thus the new manager's exploration and probing is likely to result in at least some change. This explanation of the change phenomenon is also consistent with the marked decrease of change after the 27- to 30-month period (a period of calmness extending at least as far as the 42-month period, the latest date for which data were gathered). In a sense, the manager has not only mastered the situation by 27 to 30 months, he has used up his newness.

Notes

1. See Appendix C for a description of these measures and how they were operationalized, as well as for disaggregated presentations of the activity data.

2. Insider successions were those in which the new manager had five or more years of experience in the industry of his new assignment.
3. See Argyris (1976, 1982); Schön (1983); Argyris and Schön (1974).
4. This pattern is consistent with the Reflective Observation stage of Kolb and Rubin's (1974) Learning Cycle theory.
5. I am using the term cognitive map here broadly to include such constructs as schema, social knowledge structure, script, frame, mental mode, representation. See Tolman (1951) for the basic definition of the term. See also Gray, Bougon and Donnellon (1985) for a broader description of the construct as a relationship among other concepts including continuity, proximity, contiguity, resemblance, implication, and causality (pp. 86 to 87).

3

FACTORS THAT MAKE A DIFFERENCE

The preceding chapter has provided a stage framework for understanding the progression of learning and action involved in taking charge. In this chapter, I shall examine several factors that influence how a manager takes charge, what kinds of actions he takes, what kinds of problems he is likely to face, and how successful he is likely to be. These include several factors of a background and situational nature, such as the new manager's prior functional experience (in manufacturing, marketing, finance, etc.), his prior industry experience (in the same industry as his new assignment or in another), and the situational adversity he faces (a turnaround or a normal succession).

The chapter will also deal with management style and a manager's working relationships as factors bearing on the taking-charge process.

Background and Situational Factors

PRIOR FUNCTIONAL EXPERIENCE: ROOTS THAT STAY

All other things being equal, prior experience, especially during the Taking-Hold stage, was the *single most powerful factor* associated with what the new manager focused on: the changes he made and the competence of his early actions.

Table 3-1 presents a comparative summary of whether a new

Table 3-1
Functional Experience and Actions Taken

| | Longitudinal Studies | | | | Historical Studies | | | | | | | | | |
| | Division Presidents | | | | Other General Managers | | | | | Functional Managers | | | | |
	1	2	3	4	5	6	7	8	9	10	11	12	13	14
Actions taken														
Initial Actions														
Initial activities were in area of prior functional experience	X	X	X	X	X	X	X	X	X	X	X	NO	X	X
First structural change affected area of prior functional experience	X	X	X	X	X	NO	NC	X	X	X	NC	NO	X	NC
Major Action														
Most significant change made in first three years affected area of prior functional experience	X	X	X	X	X	X	X	X	X	X	X	NO	X	X
Most significant structural change affected area of prior functional experience	X	X	X	X	X	X	NC	X	X	X	NC	X	X	NC

X = yes; NO = no; NC = no change made: manager made no structural changes.

The supplementary case studies (cases 15, 16, and 17) are not included here as they focused on specific time periods rather than the entire process. See Table 1-1, chapter 1 for a summary description of each of these 14 cases.

manager's initial actions or major changes involved his areas of prior functional expertise. The Table shows that with very few exceptions the new manager's actions were in those areas in which he had the greatest prior functional expertise. This applied not only to his initial actions during the Taking-Hold stage, but in many cases to subsequent major actions that typically occurred in the Reshaping stage. That this pattern should hold for functional managers is not surprising. But that it should be as strong for the division presidents and other general managers in the study is more revealing, and indicates the extent to which experience influences competencies and points of view.

A few qualifications should be stated at this point. First, the simple summary of Table 3-1 both overstates and understates the degree to which the new manager's prior functional experience influences the actions he takes. A more detailed and thorough presentation of the new manager's major areas of involvement and actions is given in Table 3-2 (for the longitudinal studies) and in Table 3-3 (for the historical studies). As a summary of these two exhibits, Table 3-1 omits certain pieces of information; for example, in most cases the new manager's initial areas of involvement were in more than one function, and the major changes he made affected more than the single function in which he had prior experience. Also, several general managers had in-depth experience in more than one function, as was true for two presidents in the longitudinal studies (cases 1 and 2 in Table 3-2) and three of the historical studies (cases 7, 8, and 13). These qualifications notwithstanding, a review of Tables 3-2 and 3-3 will show the persistent pattern reflected in Table 3-1.

On the other hand, Table 3-1 *understates* both the specificity and pervasiveness of how much the new manager draws from his past experience in the actions he takes as he takes charge, a sense that one easily gathers from the more detailed information presented in Tables 3-2 and 3-3. For example, the former international vice president who as a new president reorganizes his division into an international/domestic structure (case 1); the president whose prior functional experience was in materi-

Table 3-2

Comparison of Prior Experience and Actions Taken, Four Division Presidents (Longitudinal Studies)

	(First 12 Months) First Major Structural Change	(First 12 Months) Initial Area of Major Involvement	(Second 12 Months) Second Area of Major Involvement	(Subunits Affected) Most Significant Structural Change	(Subunits Affected) Second Most Significant Structural Change Made
(1) Industrial and Office Products Division					
Functional Experience (earliest to most recent) Sales Marketing International operations	Reorganize firm from functional to geographic form with a domestic-international split	Bringing about the domestic international reorganization	Marketing and sales	Reorganize from functional into geographic structure with a domestic-international split **Major Areas Affected** Marketing and sales Manufacturing	Reorganize domestic sales and marketing organization **Major Areas Affected** Marketing Sales
Two Previous Assignments (most to least recent) Group VP (general management) Vice president—international (in his own division)					
Prior Organizational Structure Functional/international Functional					

42

(continued)

Table 3-2

Comparison of Prior Experience and Actions Taken, Four Division Presidents (Longitudinal Studies)

(continued)

(2) Machine-Tool Division

Functional Experience Sales Marketing Manufacturing **Two Previous Assignments** EVP for manufacturing, marketing, and sales (machine parts) VP sales and marketing (same firm) (previously VP sales in a consumer products company) **Prior Organizational Structure** Functional	Functionalizes marketing and engineering (but leaves rest of organization by product divisions)	Production planning and scheduling Cost control/business planning Pricing Acted as VP sales from month 5 through month 12	Manufacturing Sales Acted VP manufacturing from month 12 through month 17	Changes company organization from product divisions to functional **Major Areas Affected** Marketing Engineering	Integrates all of remaining operations into functional structure **Major Areas Affected** Engineering Marketing Manufacturing

(3) Consumer-Products Division

Functional Experience Sales Marketing **Two Previous Assignments** Division president (office equipment) Division president (capital goods) **Prior Organizational Structures** Divisional by product Functional	Marketing and sales of one of three subsidiaries reports directly to him; begins de facto centralization of sales and marketing	Cost reduction/control Merchandising, sales, and marketing Product line review Thins line down	Sales and marketing Corporate planning strategic analysis (acts as VP marketing from month 8 through month 16)	Changed product to functional organization, combining all divisional sales forces; coordinated marketing, *but* manufacturing not fully functionalized during the first 3 years **Major Areas Affected** Marketing and sales Merchandising	None—others were further implementation or consolidation of the first changes made

(continued)

Table 3-2
Comparison of Prior Experience and Actions Taken, Four Division Presidents (Longitudinal Studies)
(continued)

	(First 12 Months) First Major Structural Change	(First 12 Months) Initial Area of Major Involvement	(Second 12 Months) Second Area of Major Involvement	(Subunits Affected) Most Significant Structural Change	(Subunits Affected) Second Most Significant Structural Change Made
(4) Construction-Products Division					
Functional Experience Contract administration Materials and production control Manufacturing	Reorganizes manufacturing by product lines Production control reports directly to him	Production planning Institutes daily production meetings Detailed product schedule systems	Engineering and sales Reduction of work force	Reorganizes manufacturing so it is split by product lines **Major Areas Affected** Manufacturing	Reorganizes engineering so it is split by product lines* **Major Areas Affected** Engineering
Two Previous Assignments Group vice president (general management) Division president (high technology)					
Prior Organizational Structures Product divisional Functional					

*Cannot take his reorganizational efforts to full product line organization because of lack of volume to support added overhead.

44

als and production control and whose first major area of involvement is in production planning and materials control (case 3); or the new marketing vice president, a former product manager, whose first major change is to create a product management function in his new company (case 10). The same direct association can be found in most of the other cases (see cases 5, 6, 7, 8, 11, 13, and to a lesser degree 9, as shown in Table 3-3).

If one considers the persistence of this effect in light of the stages, the pattern is not so surprising: a manager's prior experience is the basis for learning and building his cognitive map when he enters his new job. Prior experience is also a good part, although not all, of the judgment base he uses in deciding what actions to take in the Taking-Hold stage, and, to a lesser degree, in the Reshaping stage. Indeed, one can argue that any significant *additional* experience base that a new manager gains as a result of taking charge of a new assignment might not occur until the Immersion stage or later.

Nevertheless, any further interpretations of the data presented in Tables 3-2 and 3-3 have to be tempered by a cause-effect dilemma. It is not possible to conclude that these new managers acted as they did only because of their prior functional experience because it is no accident that they were chosen for the assignments they were given. One would assume that they were selected, at least in part, because someone believed that their prior experience base *was* relevant to the new assignment and that they would use that knowledge in the new situation (although, as the next section will explain, lack of industry-specific experience was more often characteristic of failed successions than successful ones).

Even with this caveat, it is foolish to ignore the pervasiveness of the influence of prior functional experience. The comments of a superior of a new division president, who was six months into his assignment, make the point well:

> One thing that bothers me is that Bill is very strongly oriented towards manufacturing and they're getting all his attention. His background is in manufacturing so it's natural. Yet this is a selling business. This is an unbelievable period of time—I've never in my

Table 3-3

Comparison of Managers' Functional Experience and Actions Taken (Historical Studies)

Business, Manager's Title, and Company Sales	Prior Assignment	Functional Experience	Initial Area of Major Involvement	Areas Affected by First Structural Change	Areas Affected by Major Structural Change	Areas Affected by Most Significant Changes of First Three Years
(5) Cable television subsidiary General manager $1.2 million	Communications engineer (in another company)	Engineering	Construction and engineering planning	Engineering installation and construction	Same	Reorganization of chief engineer's department affecting engineering, construction, and installation
(10) Wholesale food distribution Vice president—marketing and sales $21 million	Vice president—marketing and planning (in another company)	Marketing and product management	Product planning and reduction of sales force	Creation of product manager's position and reorganization of product sales groups	Marketing (creation of product manager's responsibilities)	Introduction of product management
(11) District sales service organization District manager $30 million	Sales service administrator (in same company)	Customer service	Sales service audit	(No structural changes made)	(No structural changes made)	Sales service training
(6) Beverage manufacturer Division general manager $80 million	Division general manager (in another company)	Marketing and market planning (also experience in two prior turnarounds as general manager)	Sales force and marketing	Sales force	Creation of marketing function and reorganization of sales force	Revision of mission scope and revamping of marketing strategy affecting marketing and sales
(7) Plastic and metal products Group managing director $100 million	Division general manager (in same company)	Manufacturing and engineering	Manufacturing rationalization	(No structural changes made)	(No structural changes made)	Manufacturing rationalization

(continued)

Table 3-3
Comparison of Managers' Functional Experience and Actions Taken (Historical Studies)
(continued)

(12) Beverage manufacturer Director of marketing and sales $110 million	Marketing and sales director (in another company)	Marketing	Sales and sales procedures and information systems	Sales force	Sales and marketing	Sales systems and procedures
(13) Synthetic fibers Director of manufacturing $300 million	Works manager (in same company)	Manufacturing and engineering	Restructuring of manufacturing management	Manufacturing	Same	Rationalization and restructuring of production operations
(8) Computer and technical products Group vice president and general manager $780 million	Group general marketing manager (in same company)	Marketing, sales operations, and engineering	Marketing and sales operations	Group staff functions (finance, controller, group support functions)	Sales operations and marketing	Restructuring of sales and marketing operations
(9) Industrial and consumer Group CEO $3 billion	Group manufacturing director (in same company)	Manufacturing management and production control (turnaround experience)	Product strategy and product planning, manufacturing operations, and production engineering	Manufacturing and production engineering	Manufacturing, product engineering, and product planning	Manufacturing operations, production engineering, quality control, and product planning
(14) Public education Administrator	Administrator (in same system)	Educational administration (turnaround experience)	School discipline, athletics and activities, accreditation, and community involvement	(Not applicable)	(Not applicable)	Discipline, academic standards, student activities, and community involvement

47

career seen a period when it's so easy to sell—but I'm sure it's temporary. I'm sure he'll have to get more involved in sales. Right at the moment, the sales managers notice the neglect. They miss the attention. And I worry about his spending all his time in manufacturing.

PRIOR INDUSTRY EXPERIENCE:
INDUSTRY INSIDERS VERSUS OUTSIDERS

A new manager's prior experience in the industry of his new organization also has a bearing on how he takes charge and what problems he faces. (An industry insider was defined as someone having five or more years of experience in the industry of his new organization.) When successions of industry insiders are compared with those of managers who came from outside of the industry, two patterns stand out. The first is that industry insiders made more changes earlier than industry outsiders, and in that respect they took hold more quickly. In terms of the three-wave phenomenon, they began with a larger first wave of action than industry outsiders, whose first wave was generally smaller than their second. Moreover, the nature of the changes industry insiders made in their first waves tended to be more basic. Fully 33 percent of all of the structural changes made by industry insiders as a group occurred during their first six months of taking charge.

The second pattern was that the number of changes made by industry insiders was greater not only in the Taking-Hold stage (where on average it was twice as great as that of industry outsiders) but throughout the entire taking-charge process. Both of these differences can be seen graphically in Figure 3-1, which presents a plotting of organizational changes made by industry insiders compared to industry outsiders for the first thirty-six months of taking charge.

If we think of the taking-charge process in terms of learning and action, these patterns should not be surprising, since industry insiders bring a more directly relevant experience base from which to learn and act, particularly during the Taking-Hold stage. They simply start off knowing much more than industry

Figure 3-1
Industry Insiders Compared to Industry Outsiders.
Average Number of Organizational Changes per Six-Month Period
Following Succession, Categorized*

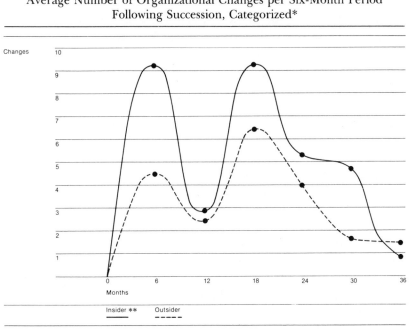

*Averages based on change data from the successful cases in the longitudinal and historical studies.
**Insider successions are those in which the new manager had five or more years' experience in the new organization's industry.

outsiders, and this advantage enables them to learn about the specifics of the new assignment more quickly and to exploit that knowledge for greater impact, not only in the early stages, but subsequently as well. Below, a subsidiary chairman describes some problems his new president was experiencing during his first year on the job:

> The problem is a new manager comes in and tends to bring in his previous experience with him. He tends to bring it in whether it's applicable or not. Jim's background is very different from this business. This business is highly competitive and low technology, while he comes from a high-tech environment where price and sales competition isn't as fierce. . . . I think a lot of his instincts are

off and it will take him a while to really understand what this is about.

The importance of prior experience is also supported by a comparison of the failed successions and those that were successfully completed. (A failed succession was defined as one in which the new manager was terminated within three years of taking charge for failure to meet top management's expectations.) Lack of industry-specific experience characterized three out of four failed successions as compared to less than half of the successful ones.

The difficulties facing an industry outsider can be illustrated by one of the failed cases. A marketing manager with over fifteen years' experience in packaged goods and toiletries became sales and marketing director of a $110 million alcoholic beverages division. On the surface, his strong marketing and product management background seemed a good fit, but his new industry was quite different from traditional packaged goods. In the new industry, the product was sold through independent distributors, mostly entrepreneurs who, though lacking marketing sophistication, were savvy and tough business people. Developing and maintaining personal relationships with key distributors was critical, because a great deal of business was done on trust. Much entertaining and personal contact, of a kind the new manager had not previously experienced, was necessary. The new manager's prior packaged goods experience served him well in product planning and in designing and implementing a number of needed systems changes during the Taking-Hold period and in later restructuring the sales force. But it had not prepared him for dealing with his major distributors or the sales force, both of which were hands-on and more sales- and promotion-oriented than analytic. By the end of the Taking-Hold stage the new manager was in serious trouble with both groups. His problems were exacerbated by a number of operational decisions concerning distributor meetings, reassignments of personnel, difficulties with collections and distributor credit problems, none of which he handled well. His prior marketing and product management experience had not prepared him for these kinds of operational and sales-oriented activities. Moreover, by the end of his first year, his cool, professional management style had alienated several key distributors to the point that the division general manager had to intervene personally in these relationships, lest these distributors be lost. This in turn further undermined the new manager's ability to develop credibility with his customers and subordinates. His new industry was simply too different from that in which he had spent his career, and he had neither the industry knowledge nor the skills base to take charge successfully.

SITUATIONAL ADVERSITY:
TURNAROUNDS VERSUS NONTURNAROUNDS

When turnaround successions are compared with normal successions, a number of differences appear. The most obvious is that turnaround managers are under greater pressure to improve performance, and they engage in making more changes while taking charge than new managers in nonturnarounds. These differences are borne out by both interview and change data.

Figure 3-2 presents a summary of organizational change activity broken out by six-month periods for the turnarounds and normal successions. Although the duration of the action waves were relatively similar for the two types of successions, the turnarounds simply involved more changes in each wave than the normal successions did, a pattern that showed up case by case. Although one might assume that turnarounds would have a shorter Taking-Hold stage because of the urgency of the situation, neither the aggregated data nor the individual case data supported this expectation.

These differences are not surprising. There are several other ways, however, in which the turnarounds differed that are not evident in the activity profiles shown in Figure 3-2. A strong theme in interviews with the turnaround managers was their awareness that some of the changes they were making in the Taking-Hold stage would have to be redone later. In one case,

Figure 3-2
Turnarounds Compared with Nonturnarounds.
Average Number of Organizational Changes per Six-Month Period
Following Succession, Categorized*

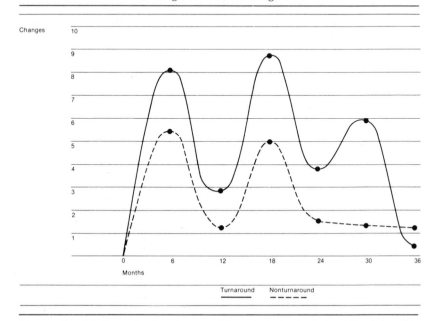

*Averages based on change data from the successful cases in the longitudinal and historical studies.

a new general manager of a $70 million consumer-products division was quite articulate about the need to implement better cost systems during his first three to five months, especially in manufacturing. But he was equally articulate about the tradeoffs involved. On the one hand, he needed better sources of information to identify specifically which products were losing money and why. On the other hand, he needed this information as soon as possible, and he knew from past experience (this was his third turnaround) that to design and implement a cost system sophisticated enough to provide all of the necessary information would take five to six months. Concluding that he simply did not have the time to do it "perfectly," he opted for a system that was simpler but easier to implement, so that he could have better, though not perfect, visibility into problems more quickly.

Suboptimal decisions were not made in ignorance but out of a need to control the situation as quickly as possible. Such actions would be improved later when the new manager and his subordinates had fewer problems to deal with, usually in the Consolidation period.

Although the turnaround managers were under substantially greater pressure than their nonturnaround counterparts, they also benefited from certain advantages. Generally, they were given much more latitude in taking action, particularly during the Taking-Hold stage. For example, a new marketing vice president of a food products subsidiary was given carte blanche by his boss and the subsidiary's parent to devise and implement a new marketing strategy. After six weeks on the job, his proposal for a reorganization of marketing was quickly approved by the subsidiary president and the parent's executive vice president. This kind of rapid approval was uncharacteristic of the nonturnaround successions.

In another case, the new general manager's parent not only gave him greater freedom in managing the $80 million division than it typically permitted its other division general managers, it buffered him from its corporate staffs for the first two years of the turnaround. The parent had several strong corporate staffs and a long tradition of corporate approval and control, especially over marketing and manufacturing. This fact was emphatically pointed out to the new manager *after* the turnaround was completed: he was told that he now had to "play by the rules" and conform more closely to corporate policies.

Similarly, the turnaround managers generally started with a larger power base than their nonturnaround counterparts because of the urgency of the situation. This was manifested in a number of ways, including the expectation that part of the new manager's mandate was to change things.

Because of the urgency, turnaround managers generally faced less rivalry and resentment from key subordinates who might have seen themselves as candidates for the job. In interviews, subordinates in the nonturnarounds who felt they had been strong candidates for their new boss's job often expressed disappointment:

> I felt dismayed not to be chosen for the job . . . of course he has the credibility of being chosen by corporate, but anyone would have that.

*   *   *

> The first problem he ran into was resistance from people who were disappointed because they didn't get the job. . . . For the first month or so there was a degree of coolness on the part of people who were [passed over]. Some, I'm sure, have thought about finding another job.

In contrast, these sentiments were seldom expressed by subordinates in the turnarounds: "The fact that we were in trouble meant there was less resentment that he was [an outsider]."

However, the subordinates' lack of resentment in the turnarounds was often replaced by a sense of fear, which several of the turnaround managers experienced as an additional source of pressure to get things settled as quickly as possible. One turnaround manager commented on his first six months:

> We're talking about a turnaround situation here . . . you go through a fear thing—no doubt about it. Regardless of what [he names several subordinates] may tell you, everybody was afraid they'd lose their job. Even my secretary was afraid. How long this lasts I don't know. When I fired [the marketing VP], I think it reestablished the fear thing. . . . It means you have to develop pockets of confidence—that people are performing at an acceptable enough rate that they don't have anything to worry about. I think this performance has also given them a new confidence, an inner confidence, that goes beyond the fear thing.

Personal and Interpersonal Factors

PERSONAL PREFERENCES AND MANAGEMENT STYLE

The background and situational factors just described are relatively easy to identify and in some cases measure. Not so easily measured, but equally important, are several factors of a personal and interpersonal nature.

One variable studied in the longitudinal studies was the new manager's management style. The managers differed significantly in how they spent their time (alone, in meetings, on tours, etc.), what kinds of meetings and interactions they preferred (one-to-one, recurrently scheduled, or specially scheduled meetings; planned meetings versus ad hoc meetings, etc.), and their preferences for formality or informality.

The manager's day-to-day style appeared to have an immediate impact on people's expectations, particularly during the Taking-Hold stage (a point elaborated further in chapter 5). The new manager's style was often a cause for major readjustments for subordinates, especially if his style differed significantly from that of his predecessor. Many subordinates described their new boss's management style as an important source of information about what he expected from them. This was most true during the Taking-Hold stage, when people scrutinized the new manager's behavior:

> I knew immediately, the first day, he was going to be different from [his predecessor]. Everyone knew he was going to be more demanding. A lot of little things—he spends no time on small talk, and whenever someone else does, he changes the subject back to business. He sits behind his desk while [his predecessor] always sat in the chair near the couch. [His predecessor] was a very informal, vague, "good Joe," seat-of-the-pants type guy. [The new president] came prepared to the teeth. We all knew it was the start of a new era.

Field observations and interviews also suggest, however, that a new manager's stylistic preferences, particularly concerning how much control he needs or how much he prefers to delegate, can affect more than just how people respond to him initially. They can influence the very process by which he takes charge, including the decisions he makes as he learns about and acts on his new assignment. In three cases, for example, managers with delegating styles expressed, as part of their rationales for reorganizations and replacements of people, the desire to delegate more to subordinates. The managers were in very different industries (synthetic fibers, industrial and office products, and consumer products), so that their preferences could not be attributed to industry contexts alone.

Perhaps the most dramatic example of a new manager's stylistic preferences influencing major organizational decisions was a new president of a $175 million division in the machine-tool and heavy equipment business. The new manager changed his division's structure from a product to a functional organization during his second year, largely because the product organization did not give him enough direct access to, or control over, the functional groups, particularly manufacturing and sales. When he first took charge, the major product groups were headed by general managers, and he found it difficult to "get visibility," as he put it, into the basic functions within each product group because of the product organization layer of management. He struggled with the division's structure throughout the Taking-Hold and Immersion stages; he continued to feel that he did not have adequate access to problems or enough control to manage the organization effectively. Finally, despite contrary advice from most of his subordinates, he decided, with the assistance of a consulting firm, to reorganize the division functionally. Implementing the change was painful for the organization and required several of his functional vice presidents to divide their time among three businesses, two of which were geographically separated, so that they had to spend part of each week traveling. Nonetheless, the change was made and the total succession was very successful.

In retrospect, one can argue that the new president might not have been as effective in taking charge had he not restructured the situation to meet his needs as a manager, regardless of the "theoretical" appropriateness of the reorganization. Indeed, during the final debriefing in the fourth year of the study, the president admitted that he felt he could not have turned the company around had he not restructured the organization to fit his management style. It is interesting, however, that after the president's departure, his successor began a series of changes which again made the organization more product-oriented.

New managers who changed their organizations to fit their management preferences were not all successful. One individual who altered his organization so he could delegate more was terminated after two and a half years, in part because he was perceived as not having a good enough grasp of the operational details and problems of his operation. So one cannot conclude that this is always a successful strategy. But at a descriptive level, one cannot ignore management style; it affects how managers take charge and influences their organizational decisions, for better or worse. For a new manager, the key question is whether changes that fit his stylistic preferences also fit the needs of the business or organization.

RELATIONSHIPS WITH KEY PEOPLE

Closely related to the question of management style is the development of working relationships. Perhaps the most salient difference between the successful and the failed transitions was the quality of a new manager's working relationships at the end of his first year. Three of four managers in the failed successions had poor working relationships with two or more of their key subordinates by the end of twelve months. (A poor working relationship was defined as one which either the new manager or his subordinate described as being dissatisfying or ineffective.) Three out of four also had poor relationships with two or more peers, and all had poor working relationships with their superiors by the end of their first year. In contrast, only three of the thirteen new managers in the successful transitions had a poor relationship with their boss at the end of that period and none had poor relationships with as many as two of their direct reports.

There were many reasons for these interpersonal problems, including unresolved issues of rivalry, conflicts over goals, differences over what constituted effective performance, and conflicts in management style. Behind all of these reasons lay the new manager's failure to develop a set of shared expectations about performance, roles, or priorities with his key subordinates or his boss. The result of this failure was either unresolved but ongoing differences in goals or vagueness in responsibility and objectives. In general, there had been a failure to clarify, test, or work through explicit expectations, which inevitably led to lack of trust in both directions. The comments of the superior of one manager who eventually failed are an example:

> We agree on general purposes but not on how to get things done. His ideas about priorities and where he should be spending his time are very different from mine. He should be spending more time in the field and coordinating better with other departments. He agrees, but I don't see him doing it. Right now, I can't trust him to follow up which means I'm second-guessing him all the time.

According to the interviews, developing effective working relationships was a critical task of the Taking-Hold and Immersion stages. Typically, agreement on basic goals would be worked out early in the Taking-Hold stage, with further elaboration, negotiation, and oftentimes conflict occurring later in the stage. In most cases, in the Immersion stage expectations were further tested and elaborated as parties came to know each other's motives, strengths, and weaknesses in more depth. However, this entire process took place much more quickly if the new manager was highly dependent on a key subordinate or if major differences appeared early on (which occurred in a quarter of the cases), especially if the subordinate's area was in trouble or questions arose about his competence or intentions (which occurred in nearly half the cases).

If important differences between the new manager and key subordinates were not addressed and explored by the Immersion stage at the latest, they typically led to further problems. In the successful transitions, such differences were usually confronted by the end of the Immersion stage and resolved either by attaining agreement or by the subordinate's leaving or being terminated.

In one of the general management successions, the new president of a consumer-products division and his marketing VP had major differences of opinion on what the sales force's role should be vis-à-vis distributors, how the sales force should be compensated, and what minimum order sizes should be for special runs. As the two men worked on these differences during the Taking-Hold stage, it became clear to both that each had a totally different idea of how to run the business. It also became clear that the VP could not commit himself to the changes the president wanted. The president finally asked for the VP's resignation. To the president's surprise, the VP expressed relief, saying that he would have found it difficult to do things he did not believe in. Both then agreed upon a transition period while the VP secured another job.

There were obviously instances in which confronting important differences led to resolution and agreement. The overall pattern was that in the successful transitions, basic differences were worked out one way or another by the end of the Taking-Hold stage or during the Immersion stage at the latest.

CONFLICTS IN MANAGEMENT STYLE

By "conflict in management style" I mean not only a difference in style but one that is a source of problems between the new manager and his boss. Nearly one-third of the new managers described such a conflict with their boss as being a major problem in taking charge.

Conflicts and differences in style also existed in relationships with subordinates. This section will focus on the problem as it pertained to the new manager and his boss, however, since this was potentially more dangerous to the new manager (it characterized, for instance, all but one of the failed successions). Whenever the problem arose, the conflict was over differences between the new manager and his boss on how "hands-on" versus "delegating" each should be in managing his area.

In one case a new general manager in a $500 million division five months into the job wanted his boss to stop a capital request that his predecessor had submitted but that the new manager wanted rescinded. The new manager was exasperated: his boss had delegated the task of reviewing the situation to his technical and financial staffs and insisted on waiting until all parties agreed that the project should be removed from the capital budget before acting. The new manager also had difficulty receiving rapid answers on operational questions from his boss, and when he pushed during staff meetings or in one-on-one sessions, the boss politely but firmly shut him off. In the manager's opinion, the boss delegated too much to his staff and was not hands-on enough, making it more difficult for him as a subordinate to take charge of his new job.

In contrast, a new vice president of marketing in a small division felt he could not get his boss off of his back. The situation finally exploded at the end of the first year when his boss gave him a poor performance review for not being involved enough in details and for delegating too much to his subordinates. The new manager retaliated by saying that his boss interfered too much and did not delegate enough to him. He further argued that if his boss would only stop meddling in his department's affairs, the operational problems his boss complained about would disappear.

What characterizes both of these situations is not just that there were differences along the hands-on versus delegating continuum, but that the differences were creating conflicts that the new manager felt impeded his ability to take charge. To some degree the conflicts were a result of the new managers' not having done enough front-end work with their bosses in working through expectations about roles, performance, and results. In some instances, such conflicts revealed a lack of fit between the new manager's style and the new situation, which, in my judgment, was true in at least three situations.

I also believe, however, such style conflicts resulted from less rational factors, including profound beliefs about what is "good" management and what is not—a good manager sets goals clearly and delegates responsibility to subordinates without interfering, or a good manager is involved in the details and is action-oriented and decisive. Style preferences also reflected some deeply rooted factors such as a person's prior managerial experience and how that had shaped his management style. For instance, in the case of the "delegating boss" just described, the manager's boss had spent most of his career in developing and selling large contracts to major customers. The contracts often took years to sell, and because the product was complex and huge sums of money were involved, it was essential that all involved parties agree on specifications and costs. It is not surprising, therefore, that the boss resisted making a quick decision on a capital budget item, delegated the staff work, and insisted that all of the relevant parties concur before taking action. In the case of the "intervening boss" all of the boss's career had been spent in smaller companies in trouble. His hands-on, intervening style was essential in those situations; that he continued to manage closely and delegate relatively little, even when managing a larger organization, is not surprising.

What can be done to deal with such differences in management style? Understanding why such differences exist is, of course, helpful, and working out in detail what one's boss expects as results can certainly make a difference. The new manager's boss is in the better position to make the situation workable for both, but in the cases I studied, the new manager was the one who had to take the initiative; he generally had to make the accommodations needed to work effectively within his superior's style. In the "delegating boss" case, for example, the new manager stopped pressing the boss with added data and arguments on the capital project and instead began working with the two staff groups to whom his boss had delegated the review.

In the successful transitions with significant style conflicts, the new managers employed similar approaches to deal with differences in style. In the three failed successions that involved style differences, the conflict escalated to the point where the relationships became untenable.

Why Successions Succeed or Fail

One important question in a comparative study of how new managers take charge is what contributes to success or failure. To the extent that the successions in this research are an indication, managers succeed or fail for a variety of reasons (including, to some degree, luck or lack of it). The findings in this chapter have already suggested several factors that either facilitated or hindered a manager's success in taking charge. With these factors in mind I shall examine more closely the differences between successful and failed cases.

PATTERNS ASSOCIATED WITH FAILURE

Table 3-4 provides a comparative summary of the successful and the failed successions* along several background, situational, and relationship dimensions. Several broad patterns are revealed.

The most prominent pattern in this comparison is that managers who failed were in more trouble as a group along these dimensions than those who succeeded. That is, they were more often industry outsiders whose prior functional experience may not have been a good fit, and *also* more often involved in problems with two or more subordinates, two or more peers or their superiors. In short, they were in more trouble from a lack of relevant background *and* their relationships with key people, than managers who succeeded.

Table 3-4 shows, however, that the failed managers did not have a monopoly on these problems. A number of the successful managers also were industry outsiders (nearly half of them), and several also had poor working relationships with their superiors. Moreover, several successful managers had conflicts in management styles with their bosses and some also had problems with peers. The difference between the two groups is that in the failed successions, the new managers were in trouble on most of these dimensions simultaneously, while in no case was a successful manager in trouble with more than three of these factors by the end of his first year.

A second pattern that stands out is that the managers who

*As mentioned earlier, a failed succession was one in which the new manager was terminated within three years of succession for failure to meet top management's performance expectations. This is a somewhat crude, but nonetheless compelling, and, I believe, realistic definition.

Table 3-4
Comparison of Successful and Failed Successions along Seven Dimensions

	Successful Successions													Failed Successions			
	1	2	3	4	6	8	9	11	13	14	15	16	17	5	7	10	12
Background/Situational																	
Industry Outsider	NO	YES	YES	YES	YES	NO	NO	NO	NO	NO	YES	NO	YES	YES	NO	YES	YES
Turnaround	NO	YES	YES	NO	YES	NO	YES	NO	YES	YES	NO	NO	YES	NO	NO	YES	NO
Prior Turnaround Experience	NO	NO	YES	NO	YES	NO	YES	NO	YES	YES	NO	NO	NO	NO	YES	NO	NO
Quality of Working Relationships by End of First Year																	
Poor working relationships with two or more subordinates	NO	NO	NO	NO	NO	NO	NO	NO	NO	NO	NO	NO	NO	YES	YES	NO	YES
Poor working relationships with two or more peers	NO	NO	NO	NO	YES	NO	NO	YES	NO	NO	NO	NO	NO	YES	NO	YES	YES
Poor working relationship with immediate superior	NO	NO	NO	NO	NO	NO	NO	YES	NO	NO	YES	YES	NO	YES	YES	YES	YES
Conflict in management style or philosophy with superior	NO	NO	NO	NO	NO	NO	NO	YES	NO	YES	YES	YES	NO	NO	YES	YES	YES

failed differed most markedly from those who succeeded in the quality of their working relationships by the end of the first year. All the managers who failed had two or more ineffective working relationships in at least two of the three categories listed. This was true in only one of the successful transitions. In addition, three out of four managers who failed had ineffective relationships with two or more subordinates by the end of the first year, while none of the successful cases fell in this category. The relationship categories distinguished more saliently between the successful and unsuccessful cases than any of the other dimensions listed, including whether it was a turnaround or even whether the new manager was an industry outsider.

What the summary of Table 3-4 does not show is why the managers in the failed cases had such problems with key people or how this factor is related to performance. It is possible that poor working relationships are a *consequence* of poor performance rather than the cause of it: that a manager who makes bad decisions as he takes charge loses credibility, thereby straining or souring his relationships with key people. Although there is some truth to this argument, the data presented in the next chapter suggest that the opposite is more likely. My interviews and observations in the failed successions indicate that a new manager's failure to develop effective working relationships with key people is more often the cause of performance problems than the result.

One reason the relationship factor is so central to the failure pattern shown in Table 3-4 is that a new manager is dependent on both his subordinates and his boss to do the learning, diagnosis, and action-taking necessary to take charge. The process is highly interactive. These relationships are particularly important for industry outsiders, who begin their successions with a number of disadvantages in experience. Thus it is understandable that the combination of being an industry outsider *and* failing to develop effective working relationships appears as a lethal pattern in Table 3-4. An industry outsider needs not only cooperation but counsel in the early stages or he runs the risk of making poor decisions and ill-informed changes.

TWO CONTRASTS

Although the comparative data just described suggest that factors such as industry experience and the manager's success in developing effective working relationships are more critical than others, none is by itself determining. In combination, however, they can indicate how much difficulty a new manager will face.

I can illustrate this point by comparing two cases which on the surface looked similar, but varied in outcome. In the first, a new vice president of marketing was brought in to turn around a regional wholesale food distributor, a newly acquired subsidiary of a large electronics and defense firm. Although the subsidiary's sales were only $21 million, the unit had become a red flag for the parent because of performance problems. The new VP arrived with an enviable track record in the consumer food products industry and was given carte blanche by the subsidiary's president and the parent's top management. In short order, he devised a new marketing strategy, implemented a major restructuring of the subsidiary's sales division, and reorganized the marketing function using a brand management concept. Margins continued to erode, however, and nine months after taking charge he was fired.

In the second situation, a new division general manager was also hired from outside the industry to turn around an $80 million beverage subsidiary that was facing serious losses. Despite his lack of experience in the beverage business, he was given considerable latitude. He formulated a new marketing strategy within his first three months, which served as a blueprint for a major restructuring of sales and marketing. He, too, reorganized along brand management lines. Within a year margins began to improve and three years later the subsidiary's sales had doubled; it enjoyed one of the largest margins in the industry.

The similarities between these cases seem striking. Both executives were in their mid-thirties and neither had prior experience in the industry of his new assignment. The two men also implemented major changes that were remarkably alike, and both worked for difficult bosses.

A number of factors worked against the new marketing vice president who was fired, however. Although he had developed a stellar track record as a marketer, he had done so in a very different environment. He had made his mark in product management with a large producer of packaged food products which enjoyed high margins and a dominant industry position. He was exceptionally skilled at using consumer advertising, sales promotion, and product planning techniques. His new firm was a small regional distributor and converter of food products, selling principally to institutional accounts in what was essentially a low-margin, commodity-like business. Moreover, unlike his previous situation, this was a turnaround. The new vice president had no experience in either a turnaround or in a small company. To complicate matters further, he worked for a difficult, "hands-on" manager who himself had no prior experience in either marketing or the food industry.

The new manager's boss and the parent (in an entirely different industry) wanted a marketing VP who was a "savior." They believed the new manager would be one and therefore gave him free reign initially. However, when the actions he took during the Taking-Hold stage failed to stem the losses, the "hands-on" boss cut back his autonomy and reduced his responsibility for major marketing decisions, which inevitably led to conflicts. The boss's actions were even less effective than those taken by the new manager, further fueling what was by now a rather strong and visible conflict in management philosophies. This precipitated further problems, resulting in the new manager being fired. The tragedy is not only that the new manager was fired, but that he was fired *just* as he was beginning to understand the business—about to enter the deeper learning of the Immersion period.

A look beneath the surface of the second case reveals a different picture. Although the new general manager had no prior experience in the beverage business, he did have a great deal of experience in turnarounds, having previously turned around two small subsidiaries for another company. He also had a background in managing both sales and manufacturing, although on a much smaller scale. His lack of industry experience was not as damaging as in the first case because the parent was in the same business as his subsidiary, and his immediate boss, the subsidiary's chairman, had over thirty years in the industry. Therefore, the new manager had knowledgeable sources of counsel to use before launching the dramatic changes he made during the Taking-Hold and Reshaping stages.

In his case, the parent was more realistic about how long it would take to turn the subsidiary around, so he was given more time than the Taking-Hold period to produce results. Moreover, although he was given wide latitude in making changes, he worked out initial expectations fairly carefully with the parent during the Taking-Hold stage and again during the Immersion and Consolidation stages. Similarly, he and his boss had also worked out a clear set of expectations early in the Taking-Hold stage, including a division of responsibilities between the two. In addition, both the new general manager and his boss were "hands-on" managers and there was not the kind of conflict that emerged in the first case, so long as each adhered to his domain. The new manager also kept his immediate boss informed and discussed proposed changes with him in detail during the early stages of his taking charge. In fact, problems did not develop in their relationship until later when the new manager became careless about informing his boss during the Consolidation stage.

Although a number of factors affect how much difficulty a new manager will face in taking charge, and it is hard to say that any one is determining, the second case shows how a new manager can minimize potential problems and compensate for his own limitations. Nonetheless, if the deck is "stacked" in terms of potential problems as it was in the first case, the findings indicate that the succession will be doomed unless the new manager or his superior is insightful enough to defuse, compensate for, or in some other way minimize the problems' effects.

IMPLICATIONS FOR SUCCESSIONS

The findings described in this chapter have several implications for succession planning and for taking charge. The first and most basic is: *a manager's prior experience and skill base make a difference and are not to be ignored in succession planning.* Although an industry outsider may bring new insights and viewpoints on problems, he does so at a cost that he and the organization will have to pay, at least in the short term. It may be important to the company to acquire these new insights, and the added learning and experience that accrue to the new manager as a result of the new assignment may add significantly to his development, but both parties need to acknowledge and anticipate the added difficulties and the time needed for the manager to have a true impact.

Perhaps the most important implication of these findings is: *the all-purpose general manager who can be slotted into just about any organization, function, or industry exists only in management textbooks.* Prior functional and industry experience does matter and it influences how a manager takes charge, the areas he is most likely to deal with effectively, and what problems he faces as he takes charge. It is foolish to expect a manager with deep experience in consumer marketing to land on his feet in an industrial marketing situation without undergoing significant additional learning which, as the findings show, does not occur overnight.

A third implication is: *success is also influenced by a number of personal and interpersonal factors,* such as management style, interpersonal skills, leadership ability, and the potential for conflicts in management style. These are less easy to grasp in succession planning and often are not dealt with as explicitly as prior functional or industry experience. Nonetheless, companies and managers who ignore these "softer" variables do so at their peril.

There are implications for a new manager taking charge as well. Given his background and skills and the specific requirements and nature of a new assignment, a new manager can safely predict what areas are likely to become challenges or problems. If his deck is stacked, he must understand this at the outset and negotiate support to pull off a difficult situation. He also needs help to overcome potential limitations especially in the early stages when most of the initial learning and preliminary action-taking occur. Finally, as the findings concerning the development of working relationships underscore, he must attend to the organizational and interpersonal work involved in taking charge.

4

THE ORGANIZATIONAL WORK
OF TAKING CHARGE

The last two chapters have described the stages new managers go through in taking charge and several factors that influence how they progress through these stages. In this chapter I will examine more closely the organizational work of taking charge, particularly as it affects the new manager's success in mastering the new assignment.

By organizational work I mean the tasks involved in assessing, developing, and improving the organization. This is distinguished from two other important aspects of taking charge. One is the interpersonal, one-on-one work of building effective working relationships with individual subordinates and superiors (the topic of the next chapter), and the other is the business-analytic and strategic work of determining business needs which, although closely related to the organizational issues I shall discuss, is beyond the scope of this book.

The organizational work of taking charge spans a range of activities, from learning how the new organization functions (who does what, how the structure and systems work, etc.) to actually changing how the organization operates (for example, by introducing new systems or altering reporting relationships). The work can be categorized or conceptualized in different ways.[1] An analysis of my own field data identified more than a dozen organizational tasks that new managers engaged in during their first twenty-four to thirty months. Here I will focus on only three of the most important:

- *Learning, assessment, and diagnosis* is the cognitive work of taking charge. It consists of learning about the organization, assessing it and its key people, and diagnosing the causes of organizational problems as well as configuring ways to improve the organization's effectiveness.
- *Working out shared expectations* is the team-building work of taking charge and consists of developing a cohesive and focused organization. An important aspect of this task is working through a shared set of expectations about priorities, goals, and standards with subordinates and superiors, and instilling them in the organization.
- *Changing the organization to improve performance* is the change work of taking charge. It involves making organizational changes aimed at improving performance.

I have chosen these organizational tasks for two reasons. First, they are descriptive of a core set of activities that occupied most of the managers during their first twenty-four to thirty months on the job, regardless of whether they were insiders or outsiders, in turnarounds or in normal successions. Second, they are the organizational activities that the successful managers as a group handled most differently from those who failed.

In practice, these tasks are not dealt with sequentially, but more or less simultaneously over time. The exigencies of taking charge of a business unit or function and the realities of how managers learn and act do not allow the new manager the luxury of working on them one at a time. The tasks are, in general, fairly straightforward; how they are accomplished is more variable. The new managers performed these activities in fairly individual ways depending on their backgrounds and styles and the situations they faced.

There are, however, several broad differences that distinguished the successful from the unsuccessful managers. As a group, the managers in the failed successions tended to work in a more isolated and less interactive fashion than the successful managers. Interviews with these failed managers, their subordinates and their superiors suggest a "Lone Ranger" approach. As a group they used such interactive vehicles as group meetings and problem-focused task forces to a much lesser degree than the managers in the successful transitions, and, as the last chapter revealed, they were not as successful in developing strong working relationships.

The broad pattern characterizing how managers who failed handled the tasks contains several elements. Their assessments and diagnoses of their new situations tended to be more narrowly focused than those who succeeded, especially during the Taking-Hold stage, so that they failed to address important organizational areas or priorities. The managers involved fewer people in their assessments and diagnoses of the organization and its problems. They were also less effective in working through shared expectations with both their superiors and subordinates in their first year on the job. All but one of the managers who failed also had difficulties in developing a cohesive management group. As a result, the changes they made, especially in the Taking-Hold stage, were less effective, either because the changes were based on partial or incorrect diagnoses of their new situations or because they were badly implemented by a management team which did not support the changes.

Learning, Assessment, and Diagnosis

The cognitive work of learning about the organization, assessing it, and diagnosing organizational problems, is a particularly important part not only of the orientational and evaluative learning of the Taking-Hold stage, when the new manager is trying to grasp his situation, but of the second stage, Immersion, when he acquires a deeper and finer-grained understanding of it.

The experienced and successful managers started this work on the first day on the job, if not earlier, while preparing for the assignment. The learning, assessment, and diagnosis occur simultaneously. The new managers' descriptions of their first weeks on the job showed that they were assessing their situations and beginning to diagnose organizational problems even as they were learning about them.[2] In some cases, the initial assessment was guided by the new manager's mandate or by questions he had raised during his preparation. Organization insiders obviously began this process with a much fuller cognitive map of the situation than organization or industry outsiders and thus they experienced less front-end learning.

ORIENTATION WORK

In all but two cases, during their first one to three weeks on the job the managers conducted a series of meetings and other activities that provided an initial opportunity for orientation and preliminary assessment. (Not surprisingly the two exceptions were insiders who had been promoted from within.) Activities included reviewing performance data, five-year plans (if they existed), touring facilities, and meeting with their new subordinates (which managers variously described as "getting to know each other," "breaking the ice," or informal "briefing" meetings). (See Appendix C, Table C-1 for a summary of these activities by case.)

This round of initial activities occurred with both industry insiders and outsiders as well as in turnarounds and nonturnarounds. Although most managers used the orientation period as an opportunity to make initial assessments, the more experienced managers also used these activities to identify patterns, spot obvious organization problems, and generate questions about areas they needed to look into further. The comments of a $70 million consumer-product-division president, for whom the new assignment was his third turnaround, give some flavor of this initial orientation work:

> The first thing I did was to meet with everyone—to say hello, introduce myself. Then I scheduled a meeting with every manager here to familiarize myself with the operations. I took notes. Put his

name down and asked him to tell me what his job was. When I met with the product planning manager and he described his job to me, I couldn't believe it! It sounded like he was running the company. But I just took notes and didn't say anything. When I met with the sales VP he told me that he didn't have authority over what products to sell—that was product planning's responsibility. I meet with a few other people and I begin to get the impression that maybe the product planning guy *was* running the company. People also found ways to say that he wasn't the easiest guy to work with either.

The VP of manufacturing told me about the manufacturing problems, but didn't know what really caused them. For example, everyone had mentioned delivery problems, so I asked him why we had them and he told me about the short runs policy [for preferred customers], and about sales selling orders on a one-shipment basis. So I began to see that a lot of the problems people were talking about were in the "mechanics" of running the business. They didn't know *how* to do things and the systems were lousy.

Then I talked with the controller and his group and I began to see some of the reasons why. All they [the controller's department] were doing was recording numbers. Plus, two of the managers in the controller's department came to me and said "I can't work for this guy." It bothered me that two of his subordinates would say that, and I don't like situations where people take a fellow apart when he's not there. But it sure raised questions about the guy.

As this quote illustrates, the manager began assessing the organization and its people and even diagnosing its organizational problems as he was still becoming oriented. He saw several patterns he felt needed further exploration: the power of product planning over other functions; the lack of attention to what he called "mechanics" (i.e., planning and control systems), and the effects of sales policies on manufacturing problems. This initial round of activities also raised questions about his controller and product planning manager. Not surprisingly, they were the first two of his direct reports whom he began to assess in depth soon afterward.

Sometimes initial assessments can be precise, depending on the obviousness of the problems and the background the new manager brings to the situation. In the case just cited, the new president identified the need for a better cost system by the end of his first week. More often, assessments based on this first round of meetings were more impressionistic, however, especially for new managers who were outsiders. Several of the more seasoned managers pointed out the dangers of making too much out of first impressions, particularly concerning people. The division president just quoted cited the following example:

> You have to be careful about relying too much on the first impression. No one could have left a better impression than Benson [a general manager who reported to him]. People at corporate thought he was the greatest thing to put on socks and my initial impressions of him were very favorable. He was bright, articulate and tough. He had presence and seemed to know his stuff. But later, when I get into exploring his area, I find we're not even playing the same ball game. Now, some of these other guys, who didn't come across so well early on, have turned out to be more solid.

EARLY ASSESSMENT AND DIAGNOSIS

After an initial round of orientation activities, the new manager's assessment and diagnosis of the situation takes shape mainly as part of the process of trying to master the assignment, or as one manager described it, of "managing it while you're trying to get your hands around it." The process may be guided by a going-in mandate, if there is one, but usually it occurs as a part of daily interactions with key people, suppliers, customers, as well as a part of the need to make decisions or to sign off on the decisions of others. In an important way, the daily litany of routine and nonroutine problems that comes with the new job are the major *arenas* in which the new manager's organizational assessment and diagnosis take place. And this learning, assessment, and diagnosing takes time, especially for industry outsiders or managers who are still inexperienced. But time is also needed for seasoned managers. One of the most experienced managers described his first six months as president of a $175 million machine-tool division:

In the early period there is a very steep learning curve. I don't really think you can be effective until you've learned. It's taken me a period of four to five months before arriving at the point that I feel I know what I'm doing—what the conditions are, the business, the people and the problems, why we weren't making money. Now I can begin to address my attention specifically to figuring out the problems. I now have the feeling that I know what has to be done and how to do a better job.

As the new manager gains experience during the Taking-Hold stage and as his cognitive map of the situation becomes fuller, his task increasingly is to diagnose the extent to which performance problems are related to organizational variables, including key people. In practice this does not happen in a neatly systematic way. Some organizational problems may become immediately apparent to the new manager even before he has been on the job long enough fully to understand the situation or develop a concept of how it should be functioning, as was the case with the division president quoted earlier. He had determined by the end of his first week that a better cost system was needed and by the end of his sixth week that his controller was incompetent. Some problems are diagnosed earlier than others depending on the prior experience and knowledge base a new manager brings to the assignment and how obvious the problems are.

Using Meetings, Systems, and Other Devices. In diagnosing organizational problems, the successful managers often used or created a number of devices for focusing on specific problems or for yielding information on their causes. Problem-focused meetings, in particular, played an important role not only for orientation but for helping a new manager and his management team diagnose performance issues (such as delivery, margin or cost problems) and their organizational implications (see, for example, Appendix C, Table C-3, cases 1, 2, and 4).

The new managers who succeeded differed from those who failed in the extent to which they engaged others in the process of diagnosing organizational problems during the first three to six months of the Taking-Hold stage, especially in their use of group-based devices. Those who succeeded used both recurrent meetings and specific problem-focused task forces or committees to a much greater degree (ten out of fourteen). In contrast, not one of the managers in the failed successions used a problem-focused task force during his first eighteen months to assess or diagnose problems (see Appendix C, Table C-1 for comparative data). This is part of the "Lone Ranger" pattern that characterized the failed successions.

New managers also used existing information and control systems to assess and diagnose organizational performance and problems. When a new manager's initial assessment showed that an existing system was inadequate in yielding the information needed to assess performance or diagnose problems, he typically responded by initiating changes in the system (or in some cases by implementing a new system) that would provide information. Systems changes were made in all but one of the longitudinal cases during the first three to six months (see Appendix C, Table C-2). With four exceptions, however, the need for major structural change (as compared to systems change) was *not* apparent to the new manager within the first three months. (Not surprisingly, two of these exceptions were managers who had been promoted from within, and a third had previously worked in the division.)

Assessing Key People. Critical to the organizational work of the Taking-Hold stage is assessing key people—their relative competencies, strengths, and weaknesses. Much of this assessment occurs naturally in day-to-day interactions. As the new manager works with key people, observes their actions, and learns more about the problems of their areas and how they handle them, early impressions become more specific and differentiated. Initial questions about a subordinate's competence, intentions, or commitment usually lead to a more explicit focus on a subordinate's performance. If differences in goals or questions about ability became apparent, the successful managers typically confronted the subordinates in question on these issues within the first three to five months in an attempt to correct the situation or, as was true in several situations, to terminate the subordinate. Failure to do this resulted in the relationship problems described in the previous chapter.

Strategic Reviews.   Whether or not a new manager and his team did a strategic review of the business also shaped the organizational assessment and diagnostic work of the Taking-Hold period. Only four new managers implemented explicit strategic analyses or reviews during their first six months. The strategic analysis either influenced the new manager's diagnosis of the organization or it led directly to organizational change. In three of these cases, the results of the strategic analysis were the basis for reassessing both the organization's structure and key subordinates.

These were, however, only a minority of the managers. Most either did not conduct a strategic analysis during their first three years (nine cases), or they did not do so until after they had taken hold of the situation and had gained at least an initial understanding of the situation (four cases).

GOING BEYOND THE INITIAL DIAGNOSES

Based on my fieldwork in the longitudinal cases, the four to eleven months that comprise the Immersion stage are critical to gaining a deeper understanding of the organization and how to improve its effectiveness. Managers typically experienced the assessment and diagnostic work of the Immersion stage as less demanding and time consuming than that of the Taking-Hold stage. Yet, in most of the successful cases, the major changes made by the new managers occurred as a result of the added understanding they acquired during this period. The underlying dynamics of why this deeper and finer-grained learning occurs have already been described in chapter 2; here I will focus on only the broad themes that characterized the second stage of diagnostic work.

Assessing the Effects of Prior Changes.   If the new manager had done a thorough job in assessing and diagnosing his situation during the Taking-Hold stage, he had developed a fairly complete cognitive map of the situation by the time he reached the Immersion stage. He now could look for patterns that had previously eluded him. Equally important, the new manager and his staff now could learn from the results of the actions and changes that they made during the Taking-Hold stage.

The possibility for further learning and diagnostic work existed whether the changes made in the earlier period were effective or ineffective in doing what the new manager had wished. If organizational changes made during the Taking-Hold stage had succeeded in dealing with the problems they were intended to address, new problems became visible. They were not previously visible because they had been overshadowed or masked by the problems that they had acted on during the Taking-Hold stage. Thus problems that were either more subtle or more basic now became clearer.

For example, the new president of a $650 million computer subsidiary and his team had reorganized the company during the Taking-Hold stage as a result of an intensive and thorough strategic analysis that occupied the new manager's first six months. This reorganization greatly reduced interdivisional conflicts and was effective in increasing the market focus of its divisions. Once these problems were eliminated, however, a number of questions became clearer about how the subsidiary's software and new-venture operations were organized. These problems had been overshadowed by the interdivisional conflicts and lack of market focus existing before the new president and his staff reorganized the company.

If the changes made in the earlier stage had *not* been effective, then the Immersion stage provided another opportunity for diagnosis. The question now became one of why these changes did not work, or why they did not have a stronger effect on performance. In the successful cases, the new managers and their staffs probed further to understand the underlying causes of the problems.

A new division president of a $55 million construction-products division and his group had diagnosed major planning and control problems in manufacturing during Taking Hold and had made several significant changes in structure and systems to correct the problems. However, during the Immersion stage it became apparent that although costs had dropped and deliveries had improved, the division was still not cost competitive. The diagnostic work of the Immersion stage was largely devoted to figuring out why. Much probing and analysis revealed that their manufacturing costs were higher than competitors' because the product's design was inherently more expensive to make, regardless of how efficiently manufacturing was managed. The new manager's probing and diagnostic work during the Immersion stage finally traced the sources of the design problems to the organization of the engineering group.

Settling Questions About Key People.   Another Immersion task is settling any continuing questions the new manager might have about key subordinates. Most managers had already dealt with obvious competence problems during the Taking-Hold stage. Not until the second six months or later did more subtle questions become clearer. It takes time for this finer-grained assessment, and, I believe, there are limits to how much a new manager can do during Taking Hold. New managers did not have an infinite store of time during their first six months and they usually focused on those areas that were either most critical or in most trouble. As a result, it was the subordinates in those areas that they got to know and assess most quickly and deeply. The time-staggered interviews of the longitudinal studies suggest that managers did not get to know subordinates in less critical areas in comparable depth until after the Taking-Hold stage was completed. Hence, nearly half of the new managers had questions about at least some subordinates well into the Immersion stage. Typically this now resulted in closer scrutiny of these subordinates; in most of the successful cases, managers confronted the subordinate with perceived shortcomings or differences in priorities or goals. The confrontations usually led to performance improvements (in four cases) or to reassignments or resignations (in three cases).

Developing Shared Expectations

The second major group of organizational tasks centers on developing and working through a set of shared expectations about goals, priorities, and roles with key subordinates and superiors. In practice, new managers begin doing this almost from their first day on the job. But developing a larger sense of shared purpose and cohesion takes considerably longer—from three to eight months, sometimes longer, in the successful cases. The new manager needs time to understand the situation, get to know his subordinates, and work out priorities, especially if he is an outsider.

Team-building work is obviously easier if the manager is an insider or if he takes over a cohesive organization that is focused on what he believes are the right goals and priorities. This was the situation in seven cases. But even under these fortunate circumstances, the task requires attention; in two of these cases, in the eyes of superiors and subordinates, the management group's cohesion and unity of purpose actually deteriorated during the new manager's first twelve months.

WORKING THROUGH SHARED EXPECTATIONS

The general pattern characterizing the successful transitions was that the new manager worked out an increasingly concrete and specific set of expectations over time, with both his direct subordinates and his boss. This often required tacit or explicit testing and in some cases negotiation of differences. The time-staggered interviews make it clear that it takes time and focus to do this, particularly during the Taking-Hold and Immersion stages. It requires an ongoing investment of time on the part of the new manager in meeting with key subordinates and superiors to work out priorities and settle differences. It also requires elapsed time: general expectations usually became more concrete and operational as a result of a number of specific interactions and decisions. In some instances, the new manager did not know enough about the situation early on to be specific about expectations and could communicate them only generally. In the successful cases, the new managers tacitly or explicitly worked at grounding general expectations in more specific and operational terms as problems were diagnosed and as the managers began to know their people better. A general manager of a $175 million machine-tool division describes his first six months:

> First of all it takes a while before you get a good enough picture of the situation to start getting specific except in the problems that are obvious to you. I tried my best from the beginning to be very firm about what we were going to do—the directions we had to move in—and as I've learned more I've become more firm. . . . But there's a changing relationship over that period. People have to learn about each other—learn how you react, do things. You learn more about them, you begin to talk more freely and with what you learn about the business, you're able to ask better questions. They become less strained, talk more freely, and you get more specific about what these directions mean. . . . You can't do all of that right away. It takes time and work.

In contrast, the prevalent pattern in the less successful transitions was either that expectations were left so general or vague that goals and priorities were still ambiguous, even after five or six months on the job, or that the new manager had failed to confront and work through important differences in expectations with key people. In one case of a small operating subsidiary, after five months the new general manager and his chief engineer still had unresolved differences over technical policy matters and equipment specifications. Their failure to resolve these differences led to considerable tension and conflict within the organization and subsequently to equipment problems. Although the problems were not given as the reasons for the manager's eventual termination, they certainly undermined his credibility in the eyes of senior management and several of his subordinates.

In another situation, the new COO of a $100 million operating group failed to work out agreed-upon performance targets with his superior and his three division general managers. Moreover, although all parties agreed in principle that organizational changes were needed in all three divisions, his division general managers complained that they could not get him to clarify what he expected, even generally. As a result, the situation felt "unmanaged" and valuable time was lost while his subordinates failed to take action. A downturn in the group's markets intensified the problems and the COO's superior concluded that his inability to deal with such obvious issues meant that he was in over his head. He was subsequently relieved of his job and transferred to another part of the parent corporation.

These two examples concern expectations about major goals and policy matters and seem dramatic because they address such large issues. However, much of the actual work of developing a set of shared expectations about how the organization should function occurs with more modest issues. In many cases, the reviews that are a normal part of managing a business provide natural arenas in which this work is accomplished. These include formal vehicles like budget reviews, capital allocation approvals, operating reports, and updates of five-year plans. All provide opportunities for expectations to be worked through and communicated.

BUILDING A MANAGEMENT TEAM

One apparent difference between the successful and unsuccessful managers was how effective they had been in building a cohesive management team. Although many arenas exist in which expectations can be worked out, one of the most important was the new manager's group of immediate subordinates. It is a natural setting in which subordinates in charge of different parts of the organization can grapple with differences and focus on common priorities.

The importance of building a well-functioning management team is obvious to most experienced managers. Several more seasoned managers were explicit about this as a major task of taking charge. The consumer-goods division manager quoted at the beginning of this chapter, who was in his third turnaround commented:

From the first few days it was obvious there was no interworking between people. And compared with the need for a standard cost system this was even more important. I can live without a standard cost system—at least for a while. But I can't turn this division around if I can't get people to pull together.

But this is a lot more subtle thing than getting a new system in place. You can't mandate that people work like a team. You can't mandate that as a priority—that is unless you're a fool. These things come subtly. People have to *want* to work together; they have to see how to do it. There has to be an environment for it and that takes time. It's my highest priority right now but I don't write it down anywhere because it's not like other priorities. If I told corporate that building a team was my prime goal they'd tell me, so what? They'd expect that as part of making things better.

A prevalent characteristic of failed successions was that the manager was viewed by subordinates and superiors as having failed to develop a cohesive management team by the end of his first twelve months. A variety of reasons were given, including lack of skill in leading people, interpersonal conflicts with direct reports, and a perception that the manager simply did not see team building as very important compared to other more pressing business problems.

Whatever the underlying causes of how the manager dealt with his subordinates, two broad patterns characterized the failed successions. The first, which occurred in half the cases, was that the manager chose not to work with his direct reports *as a group*, but individually or through formal communications. Thus many common and group-wide issues were handled largely one-on-one. Staff meetings, when they did occur, were described by subordinates as perfunctory and not very useful. Lack of group identity further worsened because even on a one-on-one basis, the new manager spent most of his time with a small number of subordinates and barely any time with others.

This pattern is another manifestation of the "Lone Ranger" theme and is, I believe, one of the causes of poor organizational assessment and diagnosis in the early stages of taking charge. It is also consistent with the failed managers' less extensive use of group-based vehicles for problem solving and diagnosis.

One of the failed cases illustrates this pattern particularly well. During his first six months the new COO of the $100 million operating group referred to earlier devoted most of his initial efforts to problems in a division he formerly headed, to the exclusion of the group's two other divisions. This caused mounting complaints of absentee management and being in the dark from the other parts of the organization. Criticisms became more hostile after his first six months because of increasing competitive pressures on all of the divisions. As a result, his division general managers became more openly critical of his lack of direction, and found occasions to voice their complaints to senior management. During this period the COO seldom met with his top managers or direct staff as a group, which further reinforced their sense of being rudderless. I also believe that the contrast between him and his predecessor exacerbated the problem. The former group COO was a highly interactive and charismatic manager who instilled strong loyalties among his management team. The comparison between his approach and the new manager's was particularly striking to people who valued being part of a team.

A second pattern that characterized cases in which new managers failed to develop cohesive management groups was an unwillingness or inability to resolve conflicts already existing within the management group. Instead, conflicts were either suppressed or left unchecked, even after five or six months. Whether this was because the new managers were preoccupied with other matters or because they had difficulty in dealing with conflicts is not clear. Whatever the cause, they did not focus on this conflict resolution or see it as a priority.

In contrast, the prevalent pattern in the successful cases was that the new manager found some way of confronting and resolving major conflicts between members of the management group and saw their resolution as important to performance. The comments of a division manager six months into a turnaround are an illustration:

> Of all the things I've said, the most important is getting people working together for a common purpose and understanding what

that common purpose is. . . . The single biggest problem in a situation like this is if you don't have a unity of purpose. Management gets fragmented, and confused—people spin their wheels. No one wants to be unsuccessful, so why does this happen?

[It's] because people can't get across to each other what needs to be done and why. . . . It all stays below the surface. When you're with a group of managers you're trying to figure out what it's all about and what *you're* all about. . . . I've never been in a situation yet where I haven't had to clear the air and get the conflicts out on the table. People tend to hold back until then. But when the air is cleared it's different. It's a tough little exercise, though, of getting the conflicts out and getting them settled. But after you've survived it, people begin to feel good with each other. Absolutely straightforward. Until you've done that, all you're doing is playing games.

Of course, building a focused and well-functioning management team is not the only way a new manager works through and communicates a shared set of expectations about goals and priorities; it is, nonetheless, important because it is through the manager's team of direct reports that he has the highest leverage in influencing the larger organization. Let me turn now to some other ways shared expectations are communicated.

SYMBOLIC BEHAVIOR

My field observations suggest that the new manager's expectations are also communicated symbolically by the actions he takes, particularly during the first three to six months of the Taking-Hold stage. One of the social realities of this period is that the new manager's behavior is the object of considerable interest to the organization as a whole—even if he is an insider. People search for clues, observing even the smallest nuances in his behavior and interpreting them.

A consequence of this heightened scrutiny is that many of the manager's routine actions symbolically communicate his expectations either intentionally or unintentionally. For example, in the case of one of the new division presidents, a number of his subordinates commented early on that he never took his jacket off except when he was touring the plant and that he had spent most of his first three months in his office. He called people to him rather than going to their offices, and he held all his meetings in his own office. At this early stage, two inferences were drawn about him and how he wanted to operate (which were widely discussed by people below his subordinates' level). The first was that he was a formal and demanding taskmaster, which was largely correct. The second was that he was not a very approachable person and did not want to waste his time with minor people or minor matters. The second, as many people later discovered, was not correct. He was a careful listener and those who worked with him found him very approachable. Yet it took time for this initial misperception to be corrected.

Even the most routine actions can communicate expectations. In two other divisions I studied, I was surprised by how many subordinates mentioned the new general manager's working hours as an example of how he had signaled expectations to the organization:

> He was the first one in the office. His car was in the lot by 7:00 a.m. every morning and he never left before 6:00 p.m. That told people a lot about what he expected from us.

The subordinate of another general manager commented:

> On Jim's arrival the message got through pretty quickly that at 8:00 a.m. he was here and come 5:00 p.m., he was still here—that he was putting in a long day—and then some. The number of people who straggled in late quickly declined. The message got across, but never a word was said.

Similarly, even how the new manager used his office or changed his furniture could communicate expectations. In one case, where a new division president was trying to break down functional barriers between departments, several of his subordinates remarked that he had replaced a rectangular conference table in his office with a circular one so that sales and manufacturing could not align themselves on opposite sides of the table. One of his subordinates commented, "You began to see that he means it." Indeed during a visit at the end of this manager's third month, I observed in the division's large conference room, a meeting of representatives from manufacturing, sales, and data processing in which the new president actually had people move their chairs so not to be seated in "blocks." As one of his subordinates said after the meeting, "You get the message he isn't kidding about breaking down functional barriers."

Both of these examples are initial impressions about general expectations, but there were similar incidents of symbolic behavior communicating more specific expectations as well. During my six-month interviews in another division, *every* member of the top management group and several people in middle management referred to an incident that had occurred two months earlier when the division had again missed its shipments quota. The new president called together the executives involved and suggested that every member of the group who was "really" concerned with the delivery problem remain in the plant until the quota had been met. By two o'clock in the morning of the next day, the quota had been shipped, and as one of his subordinates phrased it, "There was no question of our being late on shipments again." This incident, which people later called the "late hour exercise," was perceived by several of his subordinates as extreme and punitive, by others as appropriate and overdue, but all agreed it had made its point. The "late hour exercise" was so powerful in its symbolic meaning that it was still being mentioned by his subordinates in interviews two years later.

RALLYING CRIES AND THEMES

Several new managers used another method to communicate expectations to the wider organization: coining a phrase that captured one or more beliefs about what they felt the organization needed and using the phrase repeatedly. In the longitudinal studies this typically did not occur until the new manager had been on the job for three to six months, having spent enough time to work through a sense of direction and priorities. These phrases served as a shorthand to signify the manager's expectations about what the organization should focus on or where it should move. They became themes or rallying cries.

For one division president the theme became "fixing the mechanics," an expression that he and his management team used increasingly as a symbol of what they were working on. In another turnaround, the rallying cry was "instilling discipline," which subsumed a whole number of expectations about better planning, the introduction of tighter control systems, and a more disciplined management of the business. The use of "discipline" was so pervasive in my interviews and in meetings I attended during this manager's second year, that there were times when I felt I was visiting a Marine Corps boot camp. The point is that it worked to communicate a whole set of expectations about how the business should be run and provided a shorthand for reinforcing those expectations.

Other examples included "decompartmentalizing," "closing the black hole," (in a situation in which severe inventory problems existed), and "making the elephant jump," (making a large organization quicker and more responsive).

The most surprising rallying cry appeared in one of the organizations that I had chosen to study because, by my criteria, it was unambiguously *not* a turnaround. The division had a long and sustained record of growth and profitability and was clearly not in economic trouble. I was therefore amused to discover on a visit during the manager's second year that his rallying cry had become, "turning the company around." Both he and his subordinates, and even his superiors, referred to what the new manager and his team were doing as "turning it around." By my criteria, and compared with other cases I was studying, this was by no stretch of the imagination a turnaround situation. Yet for that organization, the expression connoted specific expectations about improving margins, increasing market share, and becoming more efficient producers and aggressive marketers. Its literal meaning did not matter.

Such rallying cries are, of course, not substitutes for the detailed, day-to-day task of working out and developing shared expectations. However, if the frequency with which these rallying cries showed up in my interviews and observations are any indication, they were certainly effective in reinforcing and communicating the expectations.

Changing the Organization to Improve Performance

The third group of tasks in the organizational work of taking charge is changing the organization to improve its performance. This is less critical in well-functioning and successful organizations than in turnarounds, and the change data presented in the previous chapter show that new managers implement fewer organizational changes in normal successions than in turnarounds.

The prevalent pattern in the successful cases was that the new managers did not make major organizational changes lightly. With the exception of insider successions and some turnarounds, major changes typically were not made until the Reshaping stage—after the new managers and their groups had had enough time to take more modest corrective actions and to do subsequent assessment and diagnostic work.

There is no clear single pattern that stands out in the failed successions concerning change, but two different patterns, each of which characterized half of the failure cases. In the first, some new managers made major structural changes during Taking Hold that were viewed retrospectively by others (and particularly superiors) as being based on inadequate or incorrect diagnoses of organizational problems. Inappropriate changes worsened the situation, perhaps because they were made too quickly, before the new managers fully understood their situations. In these cases, the pattern was confounded because these managers were industry outsiders who also had difficulties working with subordinates, peers, or bosses. Thus it is quite possible that they were at a disadvantage in experience and that their "Lone Ranger" styles may have prevented them from getting useful input in diagnosing the organizational problems that the changes were intended to correct.

The pattern that characterized the other half of the failed successions was the opposite of inappropriate or premature change: the managers were perceived as either waiting too long to implement corrective changes or they failed to address serious organizational problems in a timely manner.

The common theme in these two patterns is that the new managers failed to deal with obvious organizational and performance problems effectively, either because of inappropriate changes or actions that were seen as inadequate. My own belief is that both patterns are closely related to poor diagnosis, lack of interaction, and poor team building. I should also add that how "appropriate" an organizational change is seen (especially by superiors) is not simply a function of economic results; it is dependent on what the expectations are. When there are differences about what needs to be done, or a lack of clarity, it is not surprising that organizational changes may be seen as inappropriate, either by superiors or subordinates.

DILEMMAS IN MAKING ORGANIZATIONAL CHANGES

The two patterns of "the wrong changes too soon" and "not enough change too late" that characterized the failed successions highlight a set of dilemmas faced by many of the managers studied, including successful ones, and were most keenly expressed during the Taking-Hold stage or toward the end of the Immersion stage.

The first dilemma was how quickly to move in making organizational changes to deal with existing problems when the sources of these problems were not yet thoroughly understood, as is often the case during the Taking-Hold stage. If the manager waits until he understands the situation thoroughly, he risks acting too slowly on important problems, thereby losing some of the advantages of the "honeymoon" period as well as valuable time. The manager may also lose credibility because he appears indecisive.

How quickly to make organizational changes preoccupied over a third of the successful managers, including three of the most seasoned executives, during their first three to six months on the job. One described the dilemma as follows:

> I know [the group VP] and the people here are waiting for me to make some changes and they're beginning to have questions about why nothing's happened yet. So I'm paying a price for taking my time on this and I'm not sure how much longer I can go before [taking some visible action]. But I do know I'm not ready yet.

Another said:

> Everyone knows we're in trouble. I made some changes early on [in the first two months] and they're waiting for the other shoe to drop. A couple of people [he names them] are getting a little up-tight about it, but I've got to get some things nailed down better before I'm ready to move.

On the other hand, if the new manager acts on his "best understanding" of the situation but without a full picture of all the variables, he risks acting prematurely and making a poor decision. He also risks making a change he will subsequently regret because he has precluded options he may wish he later had, particularly after the deeper learning and diagnoses of the Immersion stage.

This dilemma is particularly salient for industry-outsider managers who, in the absence of good counsel, advice, or data, may be better off deferring major changes until they have gone through the deeper learning of Immersion. That outsider successions typically had small first waves of action and large second waves probably reflects an intuitive recognition of this dilemma. The best solution for an outsider is to acquire the needed data and to involve knowledgeable others in the diagnosis of the problems and in evaluating the effectiveness of alternative ways of dealing with them.

The timing dilemma can also reappear at the end of Immersion. Since this stage typically led to a second wave of action, many managers were again concerned with how quickly to act on the added learning and experience acquired during this period. The president of a $650 million computer products subsidiary (who had implemented a major change at the seven-month period) described the tradeoff between acting on what he and his divisional management group had learned during the nine months since he had restructured the organization and the need to ensure that the organization was ready for another wave of significant change. He accurately recognized the frustration building in several of his direct reports who were convinced that further changes were needed quickly. He was also cognizant of the need to gain acceptance for these changes, especially because the division had already undergone so much change. In another case, a division president turning around a $175 million capital goods division was afraid that if he deferred restructuring the division too long he would not only lose valuable time but would become, in his words, "too cozy with the problems." He explained:

> You have to understand the problems to know what changes are needed. But if you wait too long you understand them too well and you begin to buy into all the reasons why you have them, and then you begin to lose your edge. Still, what I'm talking about here is a major reorganization and it needs to be right. That's why I've got [a consulting firm] in here to make sure I'm not going off half cocked.

The common theme in these comments is again timing. Managers handled the dilemma either by making the change and taking the risk that the timing was too fast and running into implementation problems later, or by deferring the change and living with the frustrations of impatient subordinates or superiors. In three cases the dilemma was resolved by the managers' convincing others that the changes should be delayed. In two other cases, the managers decided that the unit was in such a crisis that the costs of not acting were higher than those of acting prematurely or incorrectly.

A final dilemma in making change is whether or not performance problems in a given area are caused by the subordinate in charge of the area or by the way in which the subordinate's job or area is structured. This was an issue for six of the managers. It was not clear to them what was cause and what was effect. There was sufficient evidence to suggest that the subordinate in question was quite competent and responsive. Yet the performance of his unit was in some way deficient and the subordinate was not able to improve it. In four of these cases the dilemma was resolved by reducing the subordinate's responsibility so that he had less to focus on, and in two situations by expanding the resources available to him. The dilemma was real in these cases because the new manager was unclear about the source of the performance problem. This was qualitatively different from the new manager diagnosing the cause to be either a subordinate's limitations or the structure itself; his concerns would then center on how quickly to make the change or how to implement it.

Pre-Succession Work

This chapter has described the organizational work new managers engage in *after* they take charge. Although I did not set out to examine the effect of pre-succession activities, my interviews showed that a new manager's pre-succession preparation made a difference in some of the problems he faced as well as how he handled them. Therefore, pre-succession work deserves some mention.

In at least six cases, the manager's preparation before starting his new assignment had an important bearing on his mandate and what his going-in priorities were. It is safe to say that one of the first tasks for a new manager *before* taking on a new assignment is to understand what top management's expectations are about the unit's performance, why he was selected for the job, what top management expects him to bring to it in experience and skills, and what their general assessment of the situation is. In practice, this was done at least to some degree through oral briefings, and, in cases involving division and group general managers, by examining financial reports, and five-year plans. In nine cases pre-succession work took place during discussions leading up to the new manager's decision to accept the assignment, with more detailed information typically provided after he had accepted it.

Understanding a predecessor's strategy and priorities is also useful, not only for substantive reasons but because such knowledge is likely to provide clues about current expectations and directions. Also, there is a contrast effect that normally occurs when a new manager takes charge. People naturally compare him with his predecessor in terms of priorities, goals, actions, and style. Meeting with one's predecessor, if that is possible, is therefore helpful. Obviously, this background information is more easily obtained by a new manager who is an organizational insider and if he was formerly a direct report of his predecessor, he generally understands the context work quite well.

Although almost all the managers found the background information useful, having a clearly defined going-in mandate from top management seemed to be much more important. By a *going-in* mandate I mean the new manager's charter for approaching the assignment. In general management successions, the going-in mandates were usually not very specific about what actions to take. They focused on more general parameters such as competitive position, market share, growth, and contribution objectives.

In several successions, some of the new manager's problems could be partly traced to an inadequate going-in mandate or to the new manager's inability to get one. In one of the failed successions in which a marketing VP of a $21 million subsidiary was fired after nine months, the company's top management failed to make explicit that its most urgent priority was to reverse a decline in the newly acquired subsidiary's margins. As basic as this priority was, it was not made clear either in discussions with the individual before he took the job or six weeks after, when he gave the subsidiary's president and the parent's executive vice president a presentation of his marketing strategy that it was more important than gaining market share. As a result, the new VP's major actions were aimed at "buying" market share, which inevitably resulted in further erosion of margins in the short term. Top management *did* want to increase market share (which is what they told the new manager before they hired him), but not at the cost of further lowering margins in the short run, a priority which he did not learn until it was too late. The fault can be laid at the feet of both top management and the new manager. The latter had not explored or pressed hard enough to discover what the parameters were for increasing market share or what the relevant tradeoffs might be. And top management had failed to make a very important expectation clear. Similar cases of unclear going-in mandates resulting in problems occurred in three other cases.

There are times, however, especially in division management successions or in turnarounds, when the going-in mandate cannot be made very specific or clear. Top management does not know the situation in enough detail or the division's environment is in such a state of turbulence that there is simply too much uncertainty to be specific, even about general expectations. But even in these situations, obtaining as explicit a mandate as is reasonably possible is important. The case of a $650 million subsidiary in the computer industry provides a good illustration. The new subsidiary president was an industry outsider and the subsidiary was in serious trouble. Its markets and technologies were in turmoil and the subsidiary's three key officers were at odds over the firm's strategic direction. Despite the inherent uncertainty of the situation the new president's going-in mandate was made quite clear: make an analysis of the industry environment, determine what business the subsidiary should be in, and shape a strategic direction. In his pre-succession discussions, he also learned that one of the reasons he was chosen for the job—he was an industry outsider—was for his "people management" and marketing skills. He discovered that top management expected him to make the subsidiary's management resolve its conflicts and work together. Keenly conscious of his lack of industry experience, he and his superiors also worked out a time frame for how long this was likely to take and got an explicit agreement that corporate would "take the heat off" the subsidiary while he took hold of the situation.

I do not want to overstate the importance of the pre-succession work of gaining background and securing a going-in mandate because other factors can be more determining. In at least five of the cases, new managers were given relatively vague initial mandates (although in three the new managers had a great deal of interaction with their superiors during the Taking-Hold and Immersion stages, typically involving three to four contacts per week). On the other hand, it is foolish to ignore the importance of these pre-succession tasks because poorly defined going-in mandates *were* a source of problems in a number of the successions.

Notes

1. See, for example, Goodman 1982; and Stiener 1983.
2. This pattern is characteristic of how experienced managers think about and work on problems. See Isenberg (1985).

5

THE INTERPERSONAL WORK
OF TAKING CHARGE

A poor relationship with one's superior or with two or more subordinates was the single most prevalent characteristic of successions that failed. In this chapter, I will focus explicitly on the important interpersonal work of developing effective working relationships with key people; the emphasis is on one-on-one relationships, not the team building work described in the previous chapter. This chapter draws mainly from interviews with new managers and their subordinates during their first three years on the job.[1]

The Importance of Working Relationships

The more seasoned managers saw the task of building effective working relationships with key subordinates as an important aspect of taking charge as well as an inherent and integral part of it. The comments of a consumer-products-division president at the end of his first year are a good illustration:

> The point is you can't separate the problem of influencing the organization from the question of influencing individuals. My interpersonal relationships *are* how I influence the company. So I've put a lot of time into working with my direct reports during this period.

This was the manager's third turnaround in twelve years and he indicated his experience taught him that forming good working relationships was a basic part of taking charge. Another division president running a $260 million office and industrial products division sounded the same theme three months into his assignment while discussing a proposed restructuring of his division:

> [But] the lines and boxes are only part of it. If you don't have solid relationships with your top people, you don't have a company. You can have the right strategy and you can get corporate to sign off on a new structure, but without the ability to work with each other at the top, you can't get anything done. That's why you've seen me spending so much time with these guys.

Both the findings in chapter 3 and earlier research indicate that the quality of a manager's working relationships are especially critical at the general management and upper functional levels. For example, Mintzberg's now classic study of general managers showed that the executives he studied spent 78 percent of their working time interacting with others and as much as 50 percent of that time with subordinates.[2]

More recent research provides further support for these findings.[3] In a study of general managers, Kotter not only found the same pattern but concluded that one of the variables distinguishing general managers with consistently outstanding performance records from the rest was their ability to develop and maintain a strong network of relationships.[4] Other studies have found that subordinates reporting good relationships with their bosses are better performers, assume more responsibility, and contribute more to their units than those reporting poor relationships.[5] The importance of working relationships is documented in study after study of managerial behavior, regardless of national culture or type of management job;[6] it is not surprising, then, that it emerges as an important factor in taking charge.

Based on my time-staggered interviews with new managers and their subordinates, the time needed to develop an effective and stabilized working relationship can vary significantly depending on how much interaction occurs. As a practical matter, not all of a new manager's working relationships develop at a comparable rate. Initially, new managers invest most of their time in relationships with subordinates who are in charge of units in obvious trouble (or the new managers deem to be most critical to the success of the organization) or with subordinates who are in charge of functions with which the new manager is experienced and interested. These relationships tend to develop most quickly. Hence, a new manager may have a fairly stabilized relationship with one subordinate after his first three months and still be exploring some basic issues with another with whom he was worked less closely.

Even with these variations, however, most working relationships are developed and stabilized (for better or worse) within the new manager's first twelve months on the job.

Development of Working Relationships

Working relationships develop (or fail to develop) along several interpersonal dimensions. When interviews with new managers and their subordinates are compared over their first two years on the job, three qualities emerge as being particularly salient to the development of effective relationships:

- *Mutual expectations.* The degree to which the new manager and his subordinate work out mutual expectations about performance, goals, priorities, and roles. This theme has already been discussed at an organizational and group level in the preceding chapter, but here the focus is on the one-on-one level and the part it plays in developing effective relationships.
- *Trust.* The degree of mutual trust that develops in a relationship, the areas this trust covers, and the extent to which it has been tested. Trust was a prevalent theme in subordinates' descriptions of how the relationships with their new managers evolved.

- *Influence.* The degree to which a new manager and his subordinate influence each other beyond that which is accorded the new manager and the subordinate by virtue of their roles.

The pattern that characterizes effective relationships is that mutual expectations, trust, and influence not only grow over time but become more concrete, tested, and grounded. In those relationships described as being less than effective or satisfying (by one or both parties), expectations were left vague, or differences in expectations were not worked out, and a solid basis of trust or influence had not developed.

Mutual Expectations

One of the most important expectations of new managers and their subordinates was, of course, performance—business goals and how they should be achieved, priorities, and standards. Expectations about roles—what each person should do in his job—and issues of autonomy and influence were also important, as were expectations about the relationship itself in terms of openness, support, and the way in which conflict would be resolved.

Comparing interviews of new managers and their subordinates over time revealed one characteristic of an effective relationship: expectations became more concrete and specific as the relationship developed. Obviously, it was first necessary to discover the other's expectations and articulate one's own before differences could be worked out. In several cases, where one or both parties perceived the relationship as being less than effective or satisfying, there had been a failure to clarify, test, or work through expectations. Examples include a subordinate who, after six months, was still not clear about his new division president's expectations, or a new general manager who had not yet been able to work out specific priorities with a subordinate.

Subordinates were keenly interested in trying to learn the new manager's expectations of them as individuals and of the organization as a whole. "What does he want?" "What are his concerns?" "What are his motives?" These were all questions they wanted answered. New managers were equally curious, but about somewhat different questions. "How good is he?" "Can I rely on him?" "Will he talk straight to me?" "What does he see as the problems?"

New managers communicated and worked out expectations in a number of ways: formally and explicitly in meetings of the entire top management group or between the new manager and individual subordinates. Meetings to prepare and review budgets, operating reports, and five-year plans also served as natural occasions for grounding expectations.

More often, however, the process occurred during day-to-day, routine interactions such as ad hoc meetings on specific problems. In interviews, both managers and subordinates indicated these spontaneous situations were the most frequent and important settings; "on-the-spot feedback" was viewed as the most effective way of clarifying expectations.

Two subordinates of a new division president of a machine-tool division interpreted his initial expectations from day-to-day interactions. The first said:

> I knew right away that he wasn't coming in to win a personality contest. He started off by asking questions across the board right down to the product manager and superintendent levels—tough, detailed questions. When I took a proposal in to him he said "Well this doesn't tell me anything. What's the return on equity? What are the business indicators?" So you go back the second time with quick ratios, cash flows, ROE, etc. . . . It doesn't take long to get it.

The second commented:

> I didn't show up for a staff meeting the second week he was here and he let me know it. So, even if *he's* busy, I make myself available. One of the first questions he asked me was "Let me see your profit plan" and he really meant plan. He then got all the VPs together on several delivery problems where we had lawsuits pending and got everyone to commit on a "tight" sheet of paper dates and targets. At first, these meetings were daily, then weekly. I learned a lot

from that. . . . You get to know what he wants from these things. He wants the nitty-gritty and he wants it buttoned down.

Although these quotes might seem harsh, my observation is that a new manager's ability to be clear and direct in developing mutual expectations is not only important to subordinates but valued by them. An excerpt from an interview with a subordinate in which he describes his relationship with his new boss after eighteen months makes this point succinctly:

> He's not an easy man to like. He's very closed about his personal life and doesn't mince any words. But he knows what he's doing and he listens. You know exactly where you stand with him and everybody appreciates that. He's the best boss I've ever had and I respect him immensely. So, if you ask me if it's a good working relationship, I have to say yes, a very good one.

Development of Trust

Trust, like mutual expectations, also takes time to develop and in effective working relationships becomes more firmly grounded and differentiated. By the end of twelve months, most new managers and their subordinates had a fairly detailed sense of those areas in which they trusted each other and those in which they did not. For example, a division president talking about his relationship with his marketing VP:

> His sense of where the market is going is excellent. Nobody's better. Nobody. But he's lousy with numbers and too optimistic. So I can't trust his forecasts, though I know his nose is right about what the trend is.

A manufacturing manager about his new division general manager after twelve months commented:

> His strategic judgment is really good—especially for someone who comes from outside the business. His calls have been correct—every one of them. He also has great judgment about people. You

can see that in how he's called it with [he names several recent appointments]. These guys are turning out fantastic in these jobs.

But his people judgment isn't so good when he has to make a quick call. This has caused me some problems because he's impulsive sometimes . . . . For example, I can't trust what he'll do when he's dealing with the union or when he gets a complaint from an hourly worker—which I wish he wouldn't do. It really undercuts the foreman. There are a zillion levels between him and the hourly people and he shouldn't let anyone who comes along with a gripe just walk in his door. He makes decisions without enough background on what the consequences are. So I try like hell to keep him away from these areas. I guess this is something I've learned since the last interview. His people judgments aren't always terrific.

As these remarks suggest, judgments about trust in working relationships become more specific based on an accumulation of interactions, specific incidents, problems, and events. A critical incident might be the discovery that a subordinate or a boss had intentionally withheld important information. Incidents like this created discontinuities in a relationship's development by calling into question whatever trust had already developed. However, most of the incidents affecting judgments of trust were based on routine everyday interactions. In an important sense, these incidents provide opportunities for the new manager and his subordinate tacitly or explicitly to test and explore the ways they can trust each other and the limits of that trust. When this kind of learning and tacit testing does not take place during the Taking-Hold or Immersion stages, the relationship that develops tends to be somewhat shallow or lacking in a real basis for trust.

As the above comments also illustrate, judgments a subordinate makes about how much and in what ways he trusts his new boss also become differentiated. A theme analysis of interviews in the longitudinal studies revealed several bases of interpersonal trust, which can be grouped into character-based and competence-based sources.[7]

CHARACTER-BASED SOURCES OF TRUST

Integrity.   I use the word integrity to refer to perceptions of a manager's honesty in the relationship. Both new managers and their subordinates used integrity in a personal and moral sense. They also used such expressions as "moral character" and "basic honesty" to describe integrity. For example, one of the new presidents said the following:

> By that I don't mean whether he'll rob a bank, or steal from the till. You don't work with people like that. It's whether you sense a person has some basic principles and is willing to stand by them.

A subordinate in another company described his new superior:

> I don't like a lot of things he does, but he's basically honest. He's a genuine article and you'll forgive a lot of things because of that. That goes a long way in how much I trust him.

Motives. Next to integrity, the most frequently mentioned basis for developing trust was what one person perceived as the other's intentions. Words used to describe this included "commitment," "posture," and "agenda." Subordinates found it difficult to trust a new manager until they had first made a favorable assessment of his motives. A subordinate in a turnaround commented:

> It was hard to trust him until I knew that his purpose was not to conduct a witch hunt and that he was willing to let us prove ourselves.

Consistency of Behavior. It was surprising how much consistency mattered to both new managers and their direct reports. They used words like reliability and predictability to describe this trait. As one president put it, "How can I rely on him if I can't count on him consistently?" One executive made a similar remark regarding his new president: "He was so consistent in what he said and did, it was easy to trust him." In contrast, a subordinate in another company stated: "The one area in which it was hard to trust him initially was his lack of predictability; he's impulsive and I'm never sure when he'll change signals on me."

Openness. I use the word here in its conventional meaning: leveling with someone and being honest in discussing problems related to the business and the relationship. Managers used such phrases as "I can count on his being straight with me," "he doesn't hide problems," or "he's not afraid to speak his piece." For subordinates of new managers, openness was a particularly important basis of trust. For example:

> He's very frank about things and you know where you stand. And you can talk openly with him. He doesn't shoot you down. He'll argue with you if he disagrees but he also listens to what you have to say. That makes it easy to go in with problems. You know he'll be frank with you and he'll listen.

Discretion. Discretion was the perception that the other person would not violate confidences or carelessly divulge potentially harmful information, e.g., "He has a big mouth so it's hard to trust him with sensitive information." A new division president discussing a subordinate at the three-months point said:

> How the hell can I trust this guy? He's the one who told [names several people in other parts of the division] about the changes. One of the plant managers called John this morning to congratulate him on the new job and said he had heard about it from Tom who heard it from him. So it's all out before we've had a chance to announce it or talk to people about it. How can he be so stupid?

COMPETENCE-BASED SOURCES OF TRUST

The sources of trust I have just described would also pertain to purely social relationships. In the development of working relationships, however, competence is an added basis of trust. In interviews, three areas of competence emerged as being important: trust in a specific area of functional competence (e.g., marketing, finance); trust in an ability to work with people; and trust in overall business judgment.

Specific Competence. I use this term to mean competence in the specialized knowledge and skills required to do a particular job.

New managers had to rely on key subordinates to run different parts of the business, and thus assessing their level of competence was important in the early stages of taking charge, particularly the Taking-Hold stage. The following comment by a new division president about his vice president of marketing after six months is an example:

> Not only could we not agree on what had to be done to improve our marketing, but I also discovered he didn't even know the basics. It was impossible for me to trust his judgment on anything.

A manufacturing vice president talked about his new division president:

> His prior record matters, but if he's to be believable, you have to think he's doing it well, that his judgment is good, that he knows how to execute, that he understands good practices. And this is different from whether you agree or disagree with what he's doing. You can agree with what he's doing, but still not trust him if you have questions about his ability to execute it.

Business Sense. By business sense I mean a more generalized competence than expertise in a specific area. In interviews, people used many different expressions to describe this type of competence including "experience base," "good head for business," "sharp common sense," and "wisdom." One new manager described one of his most trusted subordinates this way:

> He sits there and listens and has the ability to get to the heart of the problem. He thinks beyond just marketing. Did you notice the questions he asked [in a meeting the researcher had observed]? They cut to the marrow. It's not just that he knows his own area well—it's more than that. It's superb common sense and an understanding of how a business works.

Interpersonal Competence. At management levels, "getting the job done" also requires competence in working with people. I use the term interpersonal competence to describe these "people skills," although none of the managers used the expression.

Nearly all, however, emphasized these people skills as an important source of trust in subordinates, easily recalling specific incidents to make their point. Said one of the new division presidents about a subordinate after eighteen months:

> I can trust him. He not only knows the business but he also knows how to work with people. He understands organizations. That's why I want him here as soon as possible in charge of manufacturing.

Subordinates also were influenced by a new manager's interpersonal competence in making judgments about trust. A subordinate described his relationship with his new manager after eighteen months:

> I have to admit, I've lost some of my trust in him since our last interview. He can be really terrible with people and that scares me. For example, he'll chew a salesman out while he's on the phone taking an order. You have to stay ahead of him all the time to be sure he isn't going to create a problem. I have to stay a step ahead of him all the time. [Gives several other examples of problems caused by the new manager's insensitivity and how this has eroded his confidence in him.]

Implicit in this subordinate's response is a judgment that at least along this dimension he has not developed trust in his new boss. The response also illustrates how trust becomes more differentiated and grounded based on specific events and interactions. Although the subordinate may be developing trust in his new boss in other aspects of their relationship, it is not occurring here. Obviously, the same dynamic of increasingly differentiated attributions applies to how new managers develop trust in subordinates.

Development of Influence

Interpersonal influence also develops (or fails to develop) in much the same way as trust and mutual expectations—over time, with each person's influence on the other increasing or waning based on a cumulative assessment of specific actions and interactions. Superior-subordinate relations are inherently asymmetric in their distribution of formal power. The new manager usually starts out with more positional power than his subordinates and less than his boss, but subordinates also have sources of power. They have the advantage of familiarity and they typically know their own area and its operations and people more intimately than their new superior.

Like trust, interpersonal influence is multidimensional and the sources of this influence can be grouped into two broad categories: (1) Those that are *positional,* bearing on the relationship (i.e., influence associated with the formal authority of an individual); and (2) those that are *personal* (i.e., influence attributed to the particular personal resources an individual brings to a relationship such as personality traits, contacts, and ability).[8]

POSITIONAL SOURCES OF INTERPERSONAL INFLUENCE

The new manager's positional bases of influence include the authority to make or recommend organizational changes, to reward and punish through salary or promotions, the power to allocate scarce resources such as budget or headcount, and the power attributed to him simply because he is the boss. These were all identified as sources of influence new managers brought to the relationship. Surprisingly, however, these positional bases of power were not viewed by either subordinates or new managers as being as important as more personal sources of influence like credibility and competence. In the third year of the longitudinal studies I asked both superiors and subordinates to rank how important the various bases of power identified in earlier interviews were as sources of *interpersonal* influence. With only occasional exceptions, positional bases of power were ranked below personal sources of influence.

PERSONAL SOURCES OF INTERPERSONAL INFLUENCE

Expertise.   For both new managers and subordinates, competence was an important source of interpersonal influence, as it was for trust. The new manager's expertise was viewed by subordinates as being more critical to a relationship than positional power; competence obviously was an important source of interpersonal influence for a subordinate as well.

Charisma or Force of Personality. Another personal source of influence mentioned by subordinates was the new manager's charisma or force of personality. Said one subordinate:

> He's really gained my confidence over these last six months. He's taken a lead in developing a relationship with me and he's on top of the details. He expresses himself strongly and he expects you to respond strongly too, one way or another. There were cases where I had made a decision that committed us to a low margin order and he just flat ass said "no—go uncommit yourself." . . . He's a very strong and aggressive person and he's very easily understood.

Another subordinate of the same manager commented:

> He's a powerful influence on me. I can't think of when I've felt more enthusiasm than over these past six months. He's a mover— doesn't believe in dallying around. There's a lot of action in working with him. He's always searching around for information and ideas. He kept calling me in to get my opinions on things so I feel I've had a big influence on his thinking, too. It's like we hit the same chord. Sometimes we're so together on things, it's a little embarrassing.

Decisiveness. Decisiveness was also seen by subordinates as a source of influence, perhaps because it contributes to an aura of competence and forcefulness and other sources of inner strength. Subordinates were quick to draw a line, however, between impulsiveness and decisiveness. A VP of engineering said of his new division president after eighteen months:

> He's had a very formal and deliberate way of taking charge— very hard-nosed in his dealings with me and everyone else. But he spent a hell of a lot of time being patient and listening. For example, [he names a $30 million project the firm was constructing for a customer]. This is a very complicated thing and he took the

time to understand it—he gets involved in the details with me. But once you need to act, he's very decisive. With [his predecessor] you never got a clear-cut answer. With Sam, you know he means business. I was ready to leave before he came and this helped change my mind. You want to work with someone who can make hard decisions.

Willingness to Use Power. A related theme described by several subordinates was the perception that the new manager was willing and able to use the power he had available if necessary. A manufacturing vice president in another division discussed his relationship with his new president after a year:

Part of his influence on me is that he's clear on what he wants and you know he's the boss. He has the gun and he's not reluctant to use it. By that, I don't mean he goes around waving it, or that he wants to use it, but you know he would if he had to. This place was a mess when he came and we knew it. I was really frustrated and a lot of us saw him as salvation. Everyone knew we were in trouble but not everyone concurred with the reasons . . . . He works at getting agreement . . . but there comes a point when you know he won't debate it any longer. Then he wants people to conform to the concept and he's shown he'll get rid of people who won't. So you take this man pretty seriously. This isn't the only reason, certainly not the most important reason, but it's one of them.

In reality, the development of expectations, trust, and influence are closely interrelated. In the excerpt that follows I had just asked a new manager why one subordinate had developed so much influence with him since he had taken charge:

Why does he influence me? Because I trust him implicitly—on every count. He doesn't distort the facts. He's a "pro" and he knows the business better than anyone else. I can rely on him to have thought through a recommendation pretty thoroughly before he makes it.

Similarly the development of trust is also influenced by how clearly mutual expectations had been worked out and by how well the new manager (or his subordinate) had met those expectations. The comments of a vice president of finance about his new division president make this point succinctly:

> Why do I have so much trust in him [his new division president]? Well, he's very clear on what he wants done and what he'll do. When we agree on something, I *know* he'll stay to his word. He's very predictable; he never surprises you . . . you know what he expects and what he will do.

This relation between trust, influence, and expectations is not surprising when we consider that most working relationships are by their very nature mutual dependencies.[9] To the extent that either party allows himself to become more influenced by the other, he also allows himself to become more dependent on the other. To the degree that this dependence is discretionary and not dictated by circumstances, it is based on the perception that the other can be trusted in that dependence.

The Interpersonal Tasks of Building Working Relationships

I have described three basic dimensions along which new managers' working relationships develop: mutual expectations, trust, and influence. But how do relationships develop along these dimensions so that expectations become mutual and a foundation of trust and mutual influence is established? Interviews suggest that these attributions develop as a result of an accumulation of interactions and events, and that in effective relationships there is a distinct trend from the general to the specific, from the vague to the differentiated. For this to occur, however, interpersonal work is needed. When one looks at this work over time it can be described in terms of a series of tasks involving orientation efforts, mutual assessment, testing, and negotiation.[10] Although these tasks occur simultaneously as two people are working together, the emphasis on each tends to change over time as a relationship develops. In this respect, the emphasis on the tasks is sequential, progressing from mutual orientation efforts toward efforts aimed at negotiating a shared set of expectations. For this reason, I will describe them in the sequence in which they generally occur.*

ORIENTATION AND INITIAL ASSESSMENT

The interpersonal work of building an effective working relationship usually begins with a brief period of mutual orientation in which the new manager and his subordinate get to know each other, each initially assessing the other from the vantage of their new roles. This typically occurs at the outset of the Taking-Hold stage while the manager is becoming oriented to the new assignment. Exceptions to this pattern occur when a subordinate is geographically distant, in which case the new manager may do this later. This initial assessment work is a mutual sizing-up that in many respects lays the groundwork for how the relationship will proceed. In effective relationships, sizing-up begins with initial first impressions and moves to more extended, less stereotyped interactions. If the manager is an outsider, much of this early activity occurs in initial early interactions when each person gives information about himself, his job, his perceptions of the existing situation—usually in briefings and one-on-one meetings. But some of this mutual orientation work also takes place in early but routine interactions.

This sizing-up happens at a time of great curiosity in both parties. Because subordinates are interested in learning about their new manager's expectations, initial encounters provide an occasion for signaling, early on, important general expectations. Subordinates are particularly sensitive to even the most subtle nuances of their new superior's behavior, and his actions often take on important meanings (sometimes beyond what is

---

*Most of this work is accomplished during the Taking-Hold and Immersion stages, though, as I said earlier, a new manager's relationships develop at different rates of intensity, so that some relationships may be quite fully developed early on, while others take longer.

warranted). Managers too are sensitive to the impressions made by their subordinates, as illustrated by the following:

> Right off, he left me with questions. He was unprepared and disorganized. Sometimes he almost sounded incoherent in trying to explain something.

Orientation work also involves an exchange of expectations, either tacitly or openly, though often this is still at a relatively general level. The manager, especially if he is an outsider, may not yet know enough either about the business or about his subordinate to initiate specific or detailed discussions. At the beginning, trust is impressionistic and highly undifferentiated unless the two people have worked together previously.

Subordinates are primarily concerned with discovering the new manager's motives and intentions. In contrast, the manager's concerns tend to focus on assessing, at least at a general level, the motives and relative competence of his subordinates. Influence is as yet relatively undeveloped beyond what is permitted to the superior by virtue of his position, and to the subordinate by virtue of his role.

Although this orientation work does not take long to complete, it is vital: it establishes general expectations about how more specific expectations will be fulfilled in the future.

Problems and Dilemmas.   One of the dilemmas for the new superior early on is how to signal appropriate expectations to a subordinate given an unfamiliarity with the job, its problems, and possibly a lack of knowledge of his subordinates as individuals. For an outsider, this dilemma is compounded because he must make decisions on the basis of recommendations made by subordinates he does not yet trust; but part of his own developing credibility depends on how well he makes those decisions.

For subordinates, a major question early on is how open and forthright to be with the new manager about problems they perceive either in their area or in the organization.

Although openness leads to building trust, a minimum level

of trust is needed before it is prudent to be open. The new manager can do the most to address this dilemma by articulating his motives (to the extent that he can) and by signaling in his own behavior a desire to confront and discuss problems openly. The simple act of soliciting information from subordinates about current problems sometimes serves this purpose. In one case, a new general manager made a point of telling each of his vice presidents he would be as honest as he could in discussing problem areas or differences and expected they would do the same. In another case (one of the turnarounds), the new president told each of his subordinates that his intention was not to "clean house," but to save the division. As he saw it, this meant identifying problems rather than hiding them. Another general manager described the process bluntly: "If you want people to be honest with you, you've got to be honest with them, and you can't be defensive when their opinions are different from yours."

A final problem that some new managers faced early on was how to deal with subordinates who may have seen themselves as candidates for his job. Typically these subordinates had ambivalent feelings toward the manager, and in some cases there were latent feelings of hostility and rivalry. The new manager has to decide how—or whether—to confront the subordinate's disappointment. Otherwise, this resentment can be an additional difficulty the new manager has to overcome in establishing a relationship with that subordinate. Such negative feelings can both affect initial sentiments and deter the development of trust and influence. This was more an issue in those units that had been doing well before the new manager was appointed than in those that had been in financial difficulty. Interviews also suggest that this tends to be a greater problem if a manager has been promoted from within.

Based on my observations, the new manager's predecessor or superior can greatly reduce this problem for the new manager by taking the initiative, preferably before the new manager has taken over, of explaining to such subordinates why they were not chosen for the job. Where this had been done, less animosity existed toward the new manager.

If one's predecessor or superior had not already addressed this issue with the subordinate, acknowledging it early in the relationship appears to work out better than not giving the subordinate the opportunity at least to express his feelings, and possible misgivings, about having been passed over.

The initial orientation work typically does not last long, and many first impressions were subsequently superseded and sometimes reversed later in the relationship as each person came to know the other better.

In summary, the major tasks of orientation work are:

- Dealing with the basic question of motives.
- Making an initial assessment of the subordinate's competence, expectations, and objectives.
- Exchanging an initial set of expectations at a general level concerning objectives, roles, and needs.
- Developing an initial understanding of how both parties will work together in the future.

EXPLORATION AND DEEPER ASSESSMENT

The next interpersonal task is gaining a deeper assessment of the other person's expectations, strengths, and limitations, so that differences can begin to surface and bases (or questions) about trust and influence can be explored. This task also begins early in the Taking-Hold stage and occurs during a period in which the new manager is still learning about the job, its problems, the organization, its key people, and its political system. It is also a period during which both parties begin to assert their identities and personal styles—who they are and what they value.

The new manager's actions continue to be scrutinized by subordinates and can have a significant influence in communicating expectations. Trust or mistrust develops as a result of this scrutiny, as each individual assesses the other's judgment, integrity, motives, competence, and consistency of actions. The subordinate explores how safe it is to be open with the new manager about problems and differences of opinion.

Working through expectations to a more concrete level requires time as well as an understanding of what the subordinate's perceptions and expectations of the situation are. One of the strong themes sounded by subordinates was that the new boss's ability to listen and understand their point of view made this expectation-setting process far easier. A subordinate described his new manager's first six months on the job:

> The first thing he did when he came was to interview the top two levels of the organization—just talking to people. Then he came back. In my case, I opened up about what the problems were and he was a real good listener. He spent a lot of time with me— sometimes we were here until 6:00 or 7:45 at night. The time wasn't important to him—he was willing to listen. I think this is why most people felt comfortable opening up to him. . . . He also kept coming back later and checking back . . .
> Also he's not all talk. . . . He'll devote a lot of time to a subject and then he asks you do you agree. . . . He asks you what do you think we ought to do. . . . So he gets you to make a firm agreement. In a way, he really boxes you in, because there are no excuses once you've agreed.

A VP of engineering in another division discussed his new superior:

> One thing that was very important to me was his just spending a hell of a lot of time being patient and listening to details. . . . He came down and became involved in understanding things his predecessor didn't have time for. . . . It's important to feel that you and your boss are talking on the same wavelength. You asked me why I didn't follow through on my resignation after he arrived. Well, this is a big part of it. You know that if you agree to something it's based on a real understanding.

Interpersonal influence also begins to develop as a result of this exploration, but somewhat tentatively. Judgments about influence are based on how much the other person has to offer and how credible he is. During this exploration, subordinates begin to assess the manager's decisiveness and credibility, sometimes adding pressure on him to take actions he is not yet certain about. If these judgments are positive, the manager's influence on the subordinate grows:

> When he first came on board, I did what he said, including some planning exercises I thought were a waste of time. I did them because he was the boss. But [the planning exercises] showed results and I could see he knew what he was doing. I'm a lot more willing to try his suggestions now.

During this period the new manager also assesses how much he should be influenced by a subordinate's recommendations and judgments:

> I had some questions about him when I first got here, but his recommendations on [X] were right on target and they showed results. I have some questions about his objectivity when it comes to recommendations on people, but I'll get a better fix on that by how he handles [his added responsibilities].

There also is some testing the limits of each person's influence. In one case, a subordinate committed the firm to an unusual contract with a supplier without prior approval of the president. This led to a confrontation between the two, after which the subordinate was forced to rescind the purchase.

The deeper exploration, which usually results in each person assessing the other's strengths and limitations, often leads to further questions. A good illustration is the division president who was turning around a $70 million consumer-products division. He had spent much time during his first three months assessing his product planning manager. He concluded that the manager's department had too much influence over other departments, but that the subordinate himself seemed very competent within his area. Now, the question was whether or not he and his subordinate could work out a new definition of responsibility acceptable to both:

> I don't know where I'll come out with him [his product planning manager]. I've cut back his influence on sales and production and we'll see how he does with planning the new line under these condi-

tions. I could have been a hero if I'd fired him the first week I was here. Everybody would have loved me for that. Nobody likes him. He's abrasive and obnoxious. But I think he's very good at [product planning]. I suspect he's the best in the industry. . . . I think there's potential there and if I can focus him on what he does well I think he will work out.

For the subordinate a major question is how open to be with the new manager; for the manager the question is how valid is the subordinate's advice and information and in what areas can he trust his judgment and competence.

Problems and Dilemmas. A major dilemma for the new manager in his exploration work is how to establish a relationship that fosters open surfacing of differences or problems, but that also succeeds in making his own standards and expectations clear. To some extent, making expectations clear and discussing deficiencies with a subordinate reinforce a climate of openness. If the new manager's comments are perceived as being too threatening, however, or if his expectations are too difficult to meet, a subordinate may suppress problems and be guarded in what he tells him. If this mutual exploration work does not address the issue, a "good-news-only" syndrome may emerge if the subordinate perceives that, despite what the new manager says, he only wants to hear that things are going the way he wants. The subordinate will then begin to avoid areas of potential conflict and will suppress differences, especially if he perceives that the manager is not open to having his own assumptions or views challenged.

The subordinate faces the dilemma of whether to be frank with the new manager about problems or differences during a period when he knows he is being evaluated by his new superior. If he fails to raise important problems or differences, he risks having his department's performance suffer. If he raises these problems or differences of opinion, he risks being seen as weak, troublesome, or incompetent. The new manager has the greatest leverage in breaking this dilemma by being open to differences of opinion, searching out problem areas, and not punishing the subordinate when he is the bearer of bad news. An engineering vice president described his boss's first six months:

> There's a tendency for people to keep bad news away from the president. But Fred got the message across that he damned well wanted to know about these problems before they came up. . . . I trusted that he meant it. Hard to say how or when. Part of it was if I had a problem I knew I could leave word, we'd talk *and* arrive at an understanding. He doesn't blow up if you bring a problem. So after a few times you begin to develop confidence that he means what he says.

If this exploration and mutual assessment work is done superficially, questions of expectations, trust, and influence may not be dealt with. When expectations are not clarified or made concrete, and trust and influence do not grow, the interpersonal "contract" that develops has the potential for causing problems later. In several cases, problems that occurred in later stages could be traced to basic expectations that had not been sufficiently explored or articulated earlier.

In summary, the major tasks of the exploration and assessment work are:

- Exploring in more detailed and concrete terms individual expectations about organizational goals, individual roles, and priorities.
- Raising and clarifying differences in expectations as they occur.
- Exploring and identifying sources of (or questions about) trust in motives, competence, consistency, and openness.
- Exploring and identifying sources of (or questions about) influence—both positional and personal—particularly in terms of credibility.

TESTING AND NEGOTIATION

Developing shared expectations requires more than the exploration and deeper assessment just described. It requires a testing of expectations and a working through of differences. Several barriers can inhibit mutual testing, including a tendency to avoid conflict on the part of the new manager or his subordinate, impatience with details, and lack of one-on-one interaction either because the new manager is preoccupied with problems with other subordinates, or the subordinate is geographically distant. In several situations where distance was an issue, the new manager made a point of visiting the subordinate or having him fly back so they could confront emerging interpersonal or performance problems face to face.

Even if the new manager is not consciously trying to test his expectations or work through differences, this interpersonal work often occurs tacitly. Some initial testing of trust and influence is part of the earlier assessment and exploration work; each party has already begun to test his own emerging expectations of what he wants in the relationship. The testing takes place both tacitly and overtly, and as a result, several core aspects of the relationship become stabilized and defined (for example, the minimal expectations each is willing to meet, in what areas trust exists, and the limits of each person's influence on the other).

Testing and negotiation can also be called a working-through period in a relationship, for now that mutual orientation and exploration has more or less been completed, unresolved issues become clearer. If prior exploration has uncovered differences in expectations or questions about them, the new manager should now attempt to resolve them or to arrive at a general agreement. To a large degree, the effectiveness of this working-through effort depends on how good a job the manager has done in the earlier tasks of clarifying and exploring expectations.

Sometimes differences must be negotiated, not just tested. Individual expectations need to be tacitly or overtly turned into mutual expectations. Important differences can be dealt with explicitly, although they are sometimes simply smoothed over because the cost of confronting them is perceived by one or both parties as too high.

For example, a senior subordinate in one company felt his

new manager was devoting too much attention to one part of the business and not enough to another. He expressed this concern, but did not press the issue, because he knew the manager was committed to improving that part of the business, while the other part was profitable. The subordinate had misgivings about the long-term consequences of the manager's priorities, but decided that pressing further was not worth the effort or the potential conflict. In another case, a division president felt that one of his subordinates was not sufficiently proactive with him or well organized. He decided not to raise these issues, however, because the department in question was a high performer and the president had other more serious problems that demanded his time and attention.

As these two examples suggest, the new manager and his subordinate made two basic assessments in determining whether to work through differences: (1) whether getting what one wants is worth the effort needed to get it, and (2) whether one is willing to live with the other's minimal expectations.

The bases and limits of trust are also defined as a result of testing and negotiation work. For example, if prior exploration has raised questions about specific areas of competence, motives, openness, or consistency, efforts can now be made to answer those questions through careful observation of the other's behavior, selective attention, or direct confrontation. The following, from a third-month interview with a new division president of a $260 million division, is an example of how these questions became sharpened:

> It became obvious to me that I just couldn't trust his judgment about equipment decisions or his honesty either. A couple of years ago he recommended we not purchase the [A] machines because of [X] problems with them and that they had been a failure in our other operations. Well it turns out they have been very effective in Italy and Sweden, and that we have had six of them in Spain for three years—which he didn't even know about! Now, when I combine that with the problems we're having with the [B] machines that we have in our domestic operations I can't help but question his judgment. Then I later find out that he now wants to order [A] type machines to replace the [B] machines. I conclude he's a man I

just can't trust. He also claims that the production data on the [A] machines was misrepresented to him. I [question that] because those production reports are in manufacturing's files and I've seen them. He either didn't bother to look, or he saw them and disregarded them.

The president then went to his file cabinet and pulled out a copy of the five-year plan. He proceeded to read sections of it written by the man in question, pointing out errors or omissions. The subordinate was subsequently demoted.

This vignette makes three points. First, it shows the accumulation of relatively routine events and interactions on which the judgments were made. Second, it is an example of the tacit and explicit kind of testing on which judgments about expectations and trust were made. Finally, it illustrates how the president differentiated his judgments in terms of his trust in his subordinate's specific competence, openness, and consistency of behavior.

Similarly, the bases and limits of influence are also tested. In effective relationships, perceptions of credibility become differentiated as a result of testing. Questions of autonomy and control are also tested with each person making tacit (and I believe sometimes unconscious) attempts to define the limits of his and the other's influence in the relationship.

When testing and negotiation of differences could not be worked out, the successful managers I studied typically confronted the subordinate in a final attempt to settle them. A new manager commented on his relationship with his marketing manager:

> We reached a point by April that was getting tense and something had to give. I was debating what to do with him. We just had too many differences about how marketing and sales should function. He was against getting wholesalers because he felt it would hurt our reputation with dealers. He also disagreed with the concept of creating product line groups, and he was very much against changing the commission structure. He never really said "that will never work," but he always did it reluctantly. Always innuendoes. So we had to have it out. And the differences were too big. In June, he decided to leave and we parted very good friends.

Several points should be made clear about the activities involved in this mutual testing and negotiation of differences. First, much of what I have referred to as testing and negotiating occurred tacitly and naturally within the context of two people working together on everyday business problems. Nonetheless, these processes were occurring, although neither party necessarily viewed himself as an adversary of the other. Second, certain expectations are defined and negotiated in a relationship before others. Typically, basic expectations about performance had been tested and defined before issues concerning influence and autonomy were settled.[11]

In summary, the interpersonal work of testing expectations and negotiating differences requires that the new manager and his subordinate work out either explicit or tacit agreements about what should be important in their relationship and what each should expect of the other. Final confrontations of differences often take place as part of this effort and are worked out by mutual accommodation, compromise, or smoothing over or through a creative resolution of differences. When attempts at resolution or accommodation fail, my observations suggest that in successful cases either the new manager or the subordinate begins to take action to terminate the relationship.

Problems and Dilemmas.   A potential problem in testing and negotiating is that the new manager may press for a resolution of differences with a subordinate prematurely—before he has had a chance to fully explore the situation and test the subordinate's judgment. When this occurs, he risks losing the subordinate (if he is wrong) and of losing credibility. The second potential problem is just the opposite: that the testing and negotiation of differences is cursory. If sufficient testing of expectations does not occur, or if mutual expectations are not clearly defined, agreement will be vague and unclear about important aspects of how the new manager and his subordinate should work together; relatively little trust or mutual influence will develop. In interviews in which this occurred, the manager and subordinate had spent little time working out differences for one of several reasons: (1) There were more pressing problems elsewhere, which demanded the manager's time; (2) geographic distance separated them; (3) one or both parties were unwilling to probe underlying issues more deeply.

Conclusion

The interpersonal work of developing effective working relationships is an important aspect of taking charge. Critical to this work is the development of mutual expectations and a foundation of trust and influence. The new manager's credibility with key people grows or diminishes as a result of how effective he is in establishing trust, mutual expectations, and influence. The pattern characterizing effective relationships is that mutual expectations move from the general to the concrete and trust and influence become both more grounded and tested. The interpersonal tasks involved in doing this include initial orientation and assessment, exploration and deeper assessment, and testing and negotiation of differences.

Situational differences can affect the problems that have to be worked out in individual relationships as well as the manner in which they are worked out. But the underlying issues and tasks in the evolution of working relationships are relatively common and predictable. The way in which these issues are worked through can make a difference in the type of relationship that will develop between managers and subordinates. Working relationships will evolve, one way or another, to be sure. But the more aware a manager is of the issues that have to be resolved to make a relationship effective, the greater the possibility that he or she will take actions that influence the direction and quality of the relationship that results.

Notes

1. This chapter draws principally from the three-year longitudinal studies although occasional references are made to the other thirteen cases. I have already published several of these findings elsewhere (Gabarro, 1978, 1979, 1986).

2. See Mintzberg, 1973, pp. 39–45.
3. See, for example, Stewart (1982) and Kotter (1982).
4. See Kotter, 1982: Chapters 2, 3, 4.
5. See, for example, Liden and Graen.
6. See Mintzberg, (1973); Gabarro (1986).
7. Perhaps the best review of research and theory on trust, particularly as related to expectations and power, is included in Walton (1968). An excellent discussion of the characteristics of trust in interpersonal relationships is given in Altman and Taylor (1973), and a comprehensive review is given by Berscheid and Walster (1969). See also, Barnes (1976) for a discussion of the development of trust in managerial relationships, and Gabarro (1986) for a review of the literature on interpersonal trust.
8. The bases of positional influence are fairly straightforward and need little elaboration; they are similar to classic typologies developed by Weber (1947), Barnard (1938), and French and Raven (1959).
9. See, for example, Kotter (1977), Dalton, Barnes, and Zaleznik (1968).
10. I have already described these activities elsewhere in a stage-paradigm form. See Gabarro (1979, 1986).
11. There were two exceptions in which issues of autonomy and influence were settled before specific goals and other expectations were worked through. In both cases, the subordinates had strong track records, and their units were highly profitable. Both subordinates were unwilling to address specific performance questions until the autonomy question was settled. I suspect they had a sufficient power base because of their past performance to insist on this autonomy.

6

MANAGING THE PROCESS
OF TAKING CHARGE

The research reported in this book offers a number of implications for managers taking charge of new assignments and for human resource personnel involved in transition management, succession planning, and career development.

1. *Taking charge takes time and effort.* The first and clearest implication is that taking charge of general management or upper-functional-level assignments takes time and effort. This raises a number of questions about the effectiveness of brief, fast-track developmental assignments at middle- and upper-levels of management.

2. *Prior experience influences effective action.* Prior functional and industry-specific experience profoundly influence the actions managers take in new assignments, the problems they are likely to face, and their relative success in taking charge. In this respect these findings challenge the myth of the all-purpose general manager who, regardless of previous experience, can be parachuted into any job in any industry or functional area and succeed without difficulty. Prior experience and specific competencies do matter and influence what a new manager brings to the assignment.

3. *People skills matter.* Competencies that managers call "people skills" also make a difference in how successfully a manager takes charge. This is particularly true of a new manager's ability

to develop an effective working relationship with key subordinates and superiors.

Finally, other human contingencies, such as management style and preferences, can also affect not just the climate the new manager creates but the organizational decisions he makes and how he implements them. The findings in chapter 3 also suggest that other "soft" contingencies, such as conflicts in management style between the new manager and key subordinates or superiors, can influence the ease and the success with which the new manager takes charge. These subjective factors often fall into the "unspeakable" category and are therefore seldom considered in succession planning decisions. Only the savviest planner factors them in with their full weight. Yet, conflicts in management style, for example, existed as problems in a number of the cases I studied and figured prominently in all but one of the failed successions.

In the remainder of this chapter, I will focus more specifically on the implications of this research for several aspects of executive succession and development. These include implications for (1) managers who are actually involved in taking charge of new assignments; (2) senior corporate executives who are concerned with managing such transitions effectively; and (3) corporate staff personnel involved in succession planning and career development.

Implications for the Manager Taking Charge

For a manager in the midst of taking charge of a new assignment this book may be a mixed blessing. On the one hand, it may be some comfort to know that taking charge is not entirely random or idiosyncratic and that it can be characterized as occurring in stages consisting of predictable learning and action agendas. On the other hand, being told that it usually takes a great deal longer than six months to a year to master a new situation may be discouraging, especially during the first three to six months when the newly assigned manager often feels overwhelmed by the amount of learning and action needed just to take hold of a new assignment.

THE PROCESS TAKES TIME

The stage paradigm suggests that the process of taking charge, as I have defined it, takes both time and effort. These stages make explicit the underlying action and learning tasks involved in mastering a new situation. The major implication of understanding these issues and stages is that they can serve as benchmarks for a new manager as he takes charge and can help in conceptualizing, at least at a general level, the nature of the learning and action involved. Most seasoned managers will find these stages intuitively familiar and characteristic of what they have gone through in mastering past assignments. The point in making them explicit, however, is to provide a basis for gauging and calibrating one's progress in mastering a new assignment and in highlighting some of the dilemmas involved.

Knowing there is more to master after the first three to seven months of the Taking-Hold stage is especially valuable when one considers that the major potential for learning and having an impact typically comes *after* this stage. Taking hold of a new assignment requires the evaluative and orientational learning and the corrective actions of the Taking-Hold stage; mastering it requires the finer-grained learning and diagnostic work of the Immersion stage and the typically more significant actions of Reshaping.

A second implication of the stage paradigm is that both learning and mastery are progressive. What is accomplished in early stages sets the groundwork for what can be achieved subsequently. This puts a particular premium on the front-end activities of the Taking-Hold stage and the subsequent probing and reflective learning of the Immersion stage. There is a "ratcheting effect": the better the job a new manager does in orienting himself and evaluating the situation, the more effective will be the corrective changes he makes during the Taking-Hold stage. Similarly, the more effective the foundation laid in the Taking-Hold stage, the better the basis for the probing and finer-grained learning in the Immersion stage. And the better the diagnostic work of the Immersion stage, the more incisive are the actions he can take during the Reshaping and Consolidation stages.

Hence, the more that a new manager can accomplish in the Taking-Hold period, the better the base for further mastery in terms of both learning and impact (that is, assuming his initial actions are not ill-informed or premature). In part this is because more of the "underbrush" has been cleared for subsequent learning and action. A good illustration is the division whose problems with channels of distribution did not become apparent until *after* the new president and his staff had reorganized the division in the Taking-Hold stage. The cross-functional problems of the original structure had been so severe that they overwhelmed and masked the distribution problems.

That all this takes time, however, can be particularly discouraging to a newly assigned general manager early in the taking-charge process. Recently I consulted with several newly appointed general managers including two new CEOs. Most were familiar with my research and felt they had progressed through the stages in previous assignments. Nonetheless, some were reluctant even to consider the possibility that it would take as long as two years to master their new assignments, even when the new assignment was a major change in industry or a major increase in scope. They felt they did not have the time to go through these stages or they were now sufficiently seasoned that they could accomplish all that was necessary in one wave of action and learning. Despite their protests, however, all were deeply immersed in preparing for a second wave of action within twelve to eighteen months.

I suspect that this reaction is both normal and necessary when a new manager is taking on a major challenge, especially a turnaround. It may be a pragmatic and a psychological necessity to approach the first six months to a year on the job *as if* there were only one crack at getting it right. Unless a new manager *believes* that he can master most of the job within a year's time, it may not be possible to generate the internal motivation necessary to do the work of the Taking-Hold and Immersion stages effectively. Both superiors and subordinates expect the new manager to start producing as quickly as possible. The danger in knowing that the new situation cannot be mastered in one wave of effort is that this knowledge might diminish the motivation necessary to do the front-end work that the Taking-Hold and Immersion stages demand. Clearly, the research reported in this book suggests that this work is not only demanding but also very critical. The function of approaching the first year as if it is "the only crack" at getting it right is that this frame of mind provides the energy necessary to do the important front-end work of taking charge.

FRONT-END WORK

Comparisons of the successful and failed successions highlight several important aspects of front-end work. One of these is developing effective working relationships with key subordinates and one's boss. The failure to do this was the most prominent characteristic that distinguished between successful and failed successions. This requires working out a set of mutual expectations about performance and roles and a tested basis for both trust and influence in the relationship. Where the new manager does not accomplish this by the end of the Immersion stage, goals remain vague or in conflict and performance suffers.

Developing effective working relationships with key subordinates always requires effort, often requires testing and sometimes negotiating specific differences. If differences in expectations develop, they need to be confronted and worked through to resolution. If this is not possible, the pattern in the successful cases is that the manager either terminates or transfers the subordinate. This may be harsh, but it is one of the most salient ways in which the successful cases differ from the failures. The same applies to the expectations worked out with a new manager's boss. In successful cases, new managers not only worked out an initial set of expectations during the Taking-Hold stage, they also made a point of keeping their superiors informed and discussed proposed changes with them in detail as they took charge. In contrast, the failed successions were characterized by vague mandates and/or a failure to gain a superior's understanding or support for important changes.

Taking charge successfully also requires that the new manager develop a set of shared expectations at the organizational level as well—particularly within the new manager's immediate group. This is the team-building work of taking charge. Among other things, this requires confronting and working out differences that exist between members of the new manager's team and developing a common focus and a sense of cohesion. One of the dominant patterns found in the failed successions is that the manager took a "Lone Ranger" approach to the new assignment in which he failed to involve his key subordinates (or boss) in the important work of diagnosing problems and building a set of shared expectations about goals and priorities. This kind of approach inevitably results in poor or incomplete diagnoses of problems (and therefore inappropriate actions or changes) or changes that are badly implemented because they do not have the support of key people.

Front-end work concerning expectations about goals, performance, and priorities is not a one-time only activity. It demands ongoing effort, discussion of problems and priorities, and the working through of differences if these expectations are to become specific enough to lead to action.

ASSESSING, CALIBRATING, AND ACTING ON PRIOR EXPERIENCE

The effects of prior experience and the role that lack of relevant background plays in failed successions also raises several implications for taking charge. Regardless of the current presumption that a professional manager's skills should be so general that he or she can go into any situation and succeed, it is important to know which strengths, relevant skills, and prior knowledge one brings to a new assignment and what one's limitations in these areas are as well. Knowing what one has to offer and what one lacks puts a number of the generic tasks of each stage in a more concrete perspective. A realistic assessment also has implications for developing an action strategy that addresses these limitations while exploiting one's strengths.

For example, a general manager of a consumer-products division was transferred to the presidency of a $650 million subsidiary in the computer industry. Although he had deep functional experience in marketing and finance, it was largely in consumer products. Both he and the parent's top management were cognizant of his lack of experience in either high-tech businesses in general or the computer industry in particular. The entire situation was complicated by the fact that the assignment was a turnaround and the subsidiary's markets were in turmoil, with competing technologies still sorting themselves out. Moreover, the subsidiary's top management group was divided on strategy, leaving the organization conflict-ridden and demoralized. The new manager's lack of industry-specific experience was an obvious drawback: the environment was changing so rapidly that he did not have the luxury of deferring major decisions for two years while he learned the ropes. Top management had chosen him for the job because of his strategic, organizational, marketing, and people skills and his general ability to get things done.

In this case both the new president and his superiors had an accurate assessment of the situation and of the strengths and limitations he brought to the job. The new president's action plan for his first six months reflected this assessment. He chose an approach which took advantage of his skills while also enabling him to learn more about the business and industry, thereby making up for his deficiencies. He knew that the subsidiary was in crisis partially because of internal conflicts over strategic direction and that it was essential to sort this out while he learned about the business. He also realized that despite these conflicts, his senior officers had industry depth. Working off of both his strategic and organizational skills, he led his top officers through a strategic analysis in which he required them to express their assumptions, data, and differences of opinion to him and to each other in terms that he could understand as an informed layman. Although some considered this a tedious approach, all of his key subordinates agreed that it had clarified the underlying issues.

This exercise, combined with a great deal of time in the field, enabled him to sort out the strategic questions while *also* learning about a technologically complex business and industry. He took further advantage of his people skills by making his senior officers confront their differences and, to the extent possible, work them through to resolution. Finally, he also drew on his organizational skills by having his top management group arrive at an organizational structure that would implement the strategy they had developed during his first five months as president. Knowing that it would take him time to get on top of the new situation, he also negotiated with corporate's top management for "air cover" as he put it, while he and his group got their house in order.

This summary leaves out a number of other actions he took, but it does provide the essence of how his approach to taking charge of the new assignment took into account both what he had to offer and what he lacked in prior experience.

Implications for Transition Management

As the preceding example indicates, there are a number of actions that top management can take to minimize potential problems for managers taking charge of new assignments. The most obvious is to make the new manager's going-in charter as explicit as possible, and where it is not possible (because top management simply does not understand the unit's business or the unit's industry is in turmoil) to make that fact known to the new manager and to arrive at some general parameters and priorities. For example, in the case of the new marketing vice president fired after nine months, the company's top management had failed to make explicit the fact that its most urgent priority was to reverse a decline in the newly acquired subsidiary's margins. As basic as this priority was, it was not made explicit to the new VP, who proceeded to take a number of actions aimed at "buying" market share, which inevitably resulted in a further short-term erosion of margins. Although top management did want to increase market share, maintaining or increasing margins was more important, at least in the short term. But this was a priority which was not communicated to the new VP until it was too late. The importance of making such priorities explicit is especially critical when the new manager's unit is in trouble.

Particularly during early stages, top management can also anticipate and minimize the potential problems a new manager may face because he lacks relevant background, by ensuring there is adequate back-up support he can tap into, either in subordinates or in corporate staffs. If there are obvious gaps in a new manager's prior experience, it is foolhardy to ignore them. It is far better to assess them realistically, as was done for the new computer subsidiary president, and to figure out how to close them.

More subtle contingencies, such as predictable conflicts with key subordinates or potential clashes in management style, are more difficult to deal with. Nonetheless, ignoring them as potential problems will serve neither the new manager nor his unit. At a minimum, they deserve to be flagged and discussed as possibilities and, to the extent possible, action-planned. If the stakes are high enough to the organization, outside help may be appropriate.

A new manager's superior can also help deal with subordinates of the new manager who saw themselves as potential candidates for his job. This problem exists at all levels but is particularly acute in upper-level successions. There is always the risk that a valuable subordinate who was passed over for the job will not only resist or impede the new manager but may also leave. Ultimately, it is up to the new manager to establish credibility with such disappointed rivals, and no one can do that for him. I believe, however, the task is made much easier for the new manager if whoever makes the succession decision explains to other candidates why the new manager was chosen. When this was done, transition for the new manager was easier and the disappointment for those who were passed over was lessened. I also believe that such an action reduces the risk of losing someone who, though passed over, is still a valuable resource.

Finally, professional resources can be made available to the new manager that help accelerate the front-end work described earlier. Companies like General Electric and Exxon have created "assimilation meetings" through which initial expectations are worked out between the new manager and his direct reports early in the succession. During meetings, conducted by human resources staff, the new manager and his direct reports can raise initial expectations, questions, and concerns early in the new manager's tenure.[1]

To begin the assimilation process, a human resource professional meets with all of the new manager's direct reports as a group during the new manager's first three weeks on the job (but without the new manager present). The purpose of this two-to three-hour session is to enable the new manager's direct reports to raise issues they feel are critical and ask questions about the new manager, his background, style, or intentions. The resource person then summarizes these issues and reports them to the new manager. Anonymity is maintained so that the subordinates need not censor their concerns. The resource person may also serve as a sounding board if the manager wishes. Usually within days, the new manager then meets with his direct reports as a group to discuss their issues and describe his own expectations.

Devices like assimilation meetings typically are made available to the new manager on a voluntary basis. To be effective they require a highly competent resource person (whether a member of the human resource staff or an outside consultant) and the assurance that confidentiality is maintained throughout. Observing this process at General Electric left me impressed. Issues that might otherwise take months for the new manager to learn or work out in the normal course of taking charge can be raised quickly; the new manager has an early opportunity to address questions of performance, priorities, and goals. Perhaps the most telling evidence of its efficacy is that in those parts of GE where this resource is available, it is almost universally requested by new managers.

Assimilation meetings are not, however, substitutes for the detailed assessment and diagnostic work or the relationship-building that are integral aspects of taking charge.

Implications for Succession Planning
and Career Development

The findings in this book also have implications for succession planning and executive development. In particular, if taking charge is defined as impact and learning, these findings raise several questions about the effectiveness of short-term assignments of two years or less at upper- and middle-management levels.

The data indicate that anywhere from two to two and a half years are needed for managers to acquire an in-depth understanding of their new situations and to translate that understanding into organizational impact. This is because the first three to seven months of the Taking-Hold stage mainly involve orientation and evaluative learning and corrective action-taking based largely on the manager's prior experience and what he is able to learn about the new situation.

Significant finer-grained learning and deeper diagnostic work does not begin until the Immersion stage when the new manager is familiar enough to probe underlying issues and learn from the consequences of the first wave of actions. Moreover, the new manager does not begin to test or act on this additional knowledge until the Reshaping stage when the added learning is translated into the second, and usually the most basic, wave of organizational changes. The Reshaping stage, however, typically does not begin until the manager's second year on the job. Finally, the manager does not consolidate these second-wave changes (or get feedback on their efficacy) until the Consolidation stage. Hence, I would argue that a new manager has not really mastered an assignment until he reaches the Refinement stage when further changes diminish and can no longer be attributed to his newness.

An implication of this pattern of learning and action is that if assignments do not last long enough for the manager to work through these stages—at least through the Reshaping stage—his impact will be limited to corrective action. The new manager will deal with those problems he knows how to approach based on his prior experience and what he has learned during the Taking-Hold stage, but not stay long enough to exploit the deeper learning of the Immersion stage. If an individual manager's prior experience is broad and deep and also appropriate to the assignment, eighteen months to two years may be sufficient. I suspect, this is unlikely. I would argue that companies looking for "quick fixes" with brief assignments at upper and middle levels will get just that. The manager will not be there long enough to deal with problems beyond those that become apparent or obvious to him based on his past experience.

I would further argue that if short-term assignments become a company policy or a de facto practice, both individual units and the organization as a whole will suffer in the long run. A de facto short-timer policy results in no one ever really taking charge in terms of dealing with long-term issues or developing an understanding that goes beyond evaluative and orientational learning. Taken to its extreme, such a policy feeds into the obsession with short-term results that Hayes and Abernathy have criticized in "Managing Our Way to Economic Decline."[2]

From a career development point of view, short-term assignments also make little sense. Most brief assignments are unlikely to last long enough to allow a new manager to progress beyond the Immersion stage, yet the payoffs to the organization in substantive change and to the individual in important residual learning and added experience do not come until later. The Taking-Hold stage involves orientational and evaluative learning in which a new manager is working largely off of his *prior* experience as shown in chapter 3. Significant additional and more reflective learning does not begin until the Immersion stage. And, as described earlier, the new manager does not have the opportunity to act on or test this learning until the Reshaping stage or evaluate his actions (and learn from them) until the Consolidation stage. Both the organization's effectiveness and the manager's development are best served by assignments that are long enough to allow the manager to progress through all five stages of the taking-charge process.

Because I have not gathered data on how many managers at these levels move more frequently than every two to three years, I cannot make any informed statements about how widespread a problem short-term assignments are. However, in my own consulting and management development experience, I hear middle-level managers frequently complain that they are not in an assignment long enough to get their arms around it. And subordinates will complain that their bosses often do not remain long enough to understand a situation in depth. I believe this problem is exacerbated if a management group is subjected to a number of short-term bosses in a row, each of whom takes corrective actions based on his past experience, but none of whom remains long enough to come to grips with more basic underlying issues. I also suspect that if the pattern continues over a long period it will breed cynicism and the belief that the corporation is interested only in short-term results.

On the other hand, one can also speculate that the findings on the learning and action stages raise questions about the costs of managers' staying too long. Although data were not gathered beyond the forty-two month period, it is striking that new managers made relatively few major changes after the twenty-seven- to thirty-month period. It may be that managers not only gain mastery as they take charge, but that they also use up their newness. If this is so, there may be disadvantages to assignments that last too long in innovation, further change, and, of course, managerial development.

The findings concerning the importance of prior experience also have implications for succession planning. The most obvious of these is that prior experience and specific competencies matter, be they technical or managerial. All other things being equal, my research suggests that an insider with industry-specific or other relevant experience is more likely to take charge with fewer difficulties than an outsider without industry-specific experience. This may sound like stating the obvious, except that one of the predominant characteristics of the failed successions was that the new managers did not have relevant experience, and these were successions that took place in well-run firms in the United States and Europe.

Under some circumstances it may be beneficial to bring in an outsider, even an industry outsider, because the organization needs new approaches or valuable skills it does not have internally. Some costs will then be paid, for one cannot expect the new manager to land on his feet running. There is simply too much situational learning to be done.

A second implication of the importance of prior experience is that it tends to challenge the concept of the professional general manager whose skills are so general that he can be dropped into any situation and succeed without difficulty.[3] Although there are turnaround specialists who do succeed in a variety of situations, they are the exception not the rule, and they are, in fact, themselves specialists of a kind: they go into difficult situations and identify those factors that have the highest leverage in bringing about improvement.

In saying that prior functional and industry experience matters, I am not arguing that general management skills do not exist or that they are not transferable across settings. I am simply saying that lack of relevant industry or functional experience will make the taking-charge process more difficult and should be considered in succession planning. For example, an industry outsider with a strong background in marketing can have a significant impact if he has subordinates or superiors who have industry depth and can complement his lack of experience as he takes charge. If these resources are lacking, however, or if it is not possible for him to tap into them—either for structural reasons or because the depth resides in people who are so nonmanagerial in their thinking that they cannot serve as good advisors or teachers—then one can predict a high likelihood of failure.

The implications I have described pose some difficult tradeoffs for career development in determining what is good for the individual, the unit, and the corporation as a whole. If a corporate objective is to develop a well-trained pool of managerial talent, then executives should be put in assignments that stretch them by broadening their experience base, either functionally or in exposure to different businesses. This will inevitably mean placing managers with less than optimal experience in charge of units whose performance may suffer as a result, at least in the short term. In cases like these, the question is whether the benefits to the individual manager and the larger organization are worth the costs to the unit involved. A related consideration arises from the fact that managers, like all human beings, learn as a result of feedback from *unsuccessful* experiences, not just successful ones; some have argued they learn even more from failures.[4] Development results from being stretched and acquiring added skills, perspective, and judgment. This takes time and means the new manager may make some mistakes as well. A corporation has to be prepared to pay these costs or at least be prepared to take the risk.

On the other hand, if a corporation always errs on the side of assigning people with strong relevant experience, another kind of cost is paid: a lack of broadening that becomes increasingly noticeable at middle and upper levels. The way out of this dilemma is to provide developmental assignments that will stretch managers but are not totally out of line with a manager's past experience and will last long enough to result in important residual learning.

Conclusion

Of the many transitions that managers make, taking charge of a new assignment is one of the most important. From a corporation's point of view, the ability to ensure effective executive successions is critical not only for continuity but for instilling vitality and promoting change. As this chapter has emphasized, senior management and corporate staff can do much to influence how successfully managers take charge in executive successions: in how they choose managers, in the clarity of the going-in mandates they give them, and in how they manage these transitions.

The taking-charge transition is also critically important to managers who are taking on new executive assignments. A bad start in an important assignment is costly—in performance and in profoundly personal ways. It can stall a career, damage a track record, and inflict the worst pain of all—failing to do what one does best. The managers who failed paid dearly in disappointment and frustration, and in the self-questioning and disorientation they experienced as a result of failing to take charge of an important executive assignment. Although all went on to new jobs and eventually gained back their self-confidence, it is fair to say they paid a steep price.

Every day, hundreds of managers take charge of executive assignments in corporations and not-for-profit organizations throughout the world. A daily skimming of *The Wall Street Journal* or the *Financial Times* will give a flavor of how ubiquitous executive succession is in business. It is a sufficiently common and important transition that it deserves to be better understood and managed.

The taking-charge transition is also very personal. As this book has shown, *how* a manager takes charge carries his or her own personal mark. Every manager is unique in background, skills, and personal style. Moreover, individual situations and the organizations that comprise them also vary greatly, so that if no two managers are alike, neither are any two situations. The process of taking charge is a highly individualistic and situationally dependent transition.

The fact that the taking-charge transition is both idiosyncratic *and* ubiquitous makes it a difficult process about which to generalize. Perhaps this is why so little has been written on it, despite its importance and pervasiveness. Although this book and the research upon which it is based has attempted to shed some light on this process, no one can offer definitive answers on a transition as multifaceted as the taking-charge process.

What this book *has* attempted to do, however, is to describe a number of the dynamics involved in the transition, and their implications for action. In the final analysis, however, the success of such transitions rests in the hands of managers themselves. To the extent that this book informs them and the senior executives and corporate staffs who appoint and support them, it will have served its purpose.

Notes

1. As a matter of historical accuracy, assimilation meetings were first developed in the U.S. Army to facilitate the transfer of command and accelerate the assimilation of newly appointed commanding officers of combat-ready units. For a specific application, see Donnelly (1985).
2. C. R. Hayes and W. Abernathy, "Managing Our Way to Economic Decline," *Harvard Business Review* (July–August 1980), p. 67.
3. The myth of the all-purpose general manager has already been convincingly challenged by Kotter in his study of general managers. C. J. Kotter, *The General Manager* (New York: Free Press, 1982).
4. See, for example, M. McCall and M. Lombardo, *The Lessons of Experience* (New York: Harper & Row, in press).

A

RESEARCH DESIGN AND METHODS

The findings reported in this book are based on a research project consisting of three sets of field studies of seventeen management successions. This appendix describes the design and methods used in each of the three field studies as well as the evolution of the research strategy and the design choices made at critical junctures of the project.

An Overview of the Three Field Studies

The first and most intensive of the three field projects was a longitudinal study of four newly assigned division presidents whom I studied over a three-year period as they went about the process of taking charge. The second set consisted of ten historical case studies of management successions in different industries. The cases were chosen to get a range of situations involving both functional and general managers, and their purpose was to expand on and verify the patterns found in the longitudinal studies. Finally, the third group consisted of three supplementary case studies that were conducted after the post hoc analysis of the longitudinal and historical studies was completed and the initial findings had been reported (Gabarro, 1983). Their purpose was to further ground and explicate the findings of the first two sets of studies.

The research approach taken in all three sets of field studies can be characterized as qualitative (Van Maanen, 1979, 1983), descriptive (Van Maanen, 1982), and interpretive (Morgan, 1983). The approach can also be described as evolutionary (Martin, 1982), since the findings of the longitudinal studies influenced the design and methods chosen for the historical studies, and the findings of both shaped the foci of the supplementary studies. For this reason, I will describe a bit of the history of how the project evolved before embarking on a more detailed discussion of the three field studies themselves.

EVOLUTION OF THE RESEARCH STRATEGY

A number of authors have described the sometimes messy and opportunistic nature of how research strategies evolve (Denzin, 1978; Van Maanen, 1979, 1983; Martin, 1982; McGrath, 1982; McGrath, Martin, and Kulka, 1982; Morgan, 1983). The history of this research project is particularly evolutionary and, to a large degree, opportunistic. It is important to note at the outset that it was not my original intention to study the taking-charge process. In fact, the longitudinal studies were not initially undertaken with this purpose in mind and the emergence of the "taking-charge" phenomenon as a subject of inquiry was an unintended consequence of the study. The original purpose of the longitudinal studies was to research the development of working relationships among senior-level managers and their subordinates. At the time, little research had been done on the development of working relationships and much of the literature on the general topic of relationship formation was based on narrowly focused laboratory experiments. My intention was to conduct a field study to observe how working relationships among managers in a company actually developed over time. I chose to study newly appointed division presidents because they provided an efficient source of newly established dyadic relationships as all of their working relationships were, by definition, new. The design also had the advantage of holding two of the variables constant across clusters of pairs: the new president and his situational context.

It was this rationale that led me to approach four newly assigned division presidents in a large, highly diversified U.S. firm. The strategy was successful in yielding thirty-two pairs of new relationships, but one of its consequences, as I will describe shortly, was that all of the parties to these relationships were centrally involved with a new president who was attempting to take charge of a division.

The need to gather data on how the new presidents were taking charge became apparent during the interviews of the first site visit. Although I had anticipated that the president's "newness" to his job would be an important context to the relationships I was studying, I had greatly underestimated how powerfully it would emerge as a theme in the first set of interviews. It was not that the new president and his subordinates were uninterested in the interpersonal dynamics of their working relationships. To the contrary, they were quite open about and keenly interested in discussing them. Rather, the relationship issues themselves were deeply imbedded in the fact of a new manager taking charge. I found it nearly impossible to understand these issues (and for the new president and his subordinates to describe them) without also discussing the new president's actions and agendas in taking charge.

Such issues as the development of trust and the working-through of differences were inextricably bound up with what the new president's intentions were, what actions he had taken in his first three months in the job, differences in goals and styles that had emerged, and how he had been learning about the situation. Furthermore, when the interviews with both the new president and his subordinates became open-ended, the content quickly moved to the broader question of how the new president was taking charge. I concluded that it would be fool-hardy to attempt to understand the development of the new president's working relationships without also trying to understand the larger context of how he was trying to take charge. Indeed, over half the content of the twenty-nine hours of field interviews from the first site visit concerned such issues as the choices facing the new president, how he was "learning the ropes," the symbolic consequences of actions he had taken in his first three months, and the business problems he and his management group were dealing with as he attempted to master the new situation.

At the conclusion of this first site visit I decided to expand the focus of the study to include the broader process of taking charge, although I still viewed it as "critical context" rather than primary focus. The other three presidents also agreed and I was able to begin my first visits to their sites with this set of dual objectives made explicit.

The original design of the longitudinal studies called for the gathering of interview and observational data only. Expanding the study's focus meant gathering two additional kinds. The first was archival and documentary, such as organization charts, announcements of organizational and personnel changes, and policy memoranda, which could provide a trace of actions taken by the new presidents as they took charge. The second kind of data related to actions and events that might not show a documentary trace but were none-theless important in understanding what the new presidents were doing as they took charge. These included such actions as the creation of a task force and the commencement of weekly production review meetings. Data about the timing and/or progress of these activities were gathered largely during the interviews, typically in the initial "up-date" portion of subsequent site visits. These two sources of additional data became the basis for the four case chronologies.

Thus, all four of the longitudinal studies were undertaken to understand both the development of working relationships and the taking-charge process. After the first eighteen months of the study, however, my efforts focused almost exclusively on the taking-charge process, for most of the working relationships had either stabilized or ended by the end of the twelve- to eighteen-month period.

The initial analysis of the longitudinal data primarily focused on the development of the thirty-two working relationships, with only a secondary focus on taking charge, which I treated as context. The findings of the initial analysis dealt principally with the development of interpersonal trust and influence as differentiated attributions, as well as the mutual testing involved in their formation. These findings have been reported elsewhere (Gabarro, 1978, 1979, 1980, 1986). Subsequent attempts to create a more elaborate and event-based analysis of the relationship-formation data, however, were frustrated by the dominance of the taking-charge issues: what I had considered "ground" (the taking-charge process) kept engulfing what I was focusing on as "figure" (the development of working relationships). This frustration ultimately led to a second analysis of the field data which looked explicitly at the taking-charge process.

The patterns that emerged from the theme analyses and the case chronologies seemed both exciting and promising, particularly the periodicity of learning themes and changes made by the new presidents as they took charge. The question was whether these patterns could be generalized beyond the four cases I had studied in depth. Hence, I undertook a second set of case studies of management successions, but one in which the sites were more diverse and the approach retrospective rather than longitudinal. The findings from these ten historical cases confirmed the patterns found in the longitudinal studies and also yielded several interesting contingencies and patterns that went substantially beyond the findings of the longitudinal studies. The third set of case studies was undertaken to understand several tasks and dilemmas that had emerged as recurrent themes in both the longitudinal and historical studies. Figure A-1 summarizes the progression of the three field studies.

Figure A-1
Evolution of the Three Field Studies

LONGITUDINAL CASE STUDIES

4 Division Presidents
Studied over Three Years

↓

HISTORICAL CASE STUDIES

10 General and Upper Functional Managers (9 Different Industries)

6 Successful Successions
4 Failed Successions

Studied Retrospectively at Three-year Period

↓

SUPPLEMENTARY STUDIES

3 General Managers (in 3 Industries)

One Studied Longitudinally over Three Years
Others Retrospectively at Six-month and Two-year Periods

With this as context, the following is a more detailed description of the three sets of field studies that comprise the present research.

The Three-Year Longitudinal Studies

The three-year longitudinal studies were the most intensive and detailed of the three sets of case studies. They consisted of four case studies of newly assigned division presidents in a large, highly diversified U.S. corporation, whose divisions varied in revenues from $55 million to $260 million and were in the construction-products, consumer-products, machine-tool, and office-products industries. All four divisions included their own manufacturing, sales, engineering, product development, and financial operations; they were, in essence, small- to medium-size companies. (See Figure A-2 for a summary of the four case sites.)

The decision to seek four division general managers from the same company was based on two considerations. First, I believed this would make the access and entry problems simpler since I would deal with

Figure A-2
The Four Longitudinal Case Studies

Turnaround Successions	Normal Successions
Machine-Tool Division	*Construction-Products Division*
—Turnaround situation	—Nonturnaround
—Predecessor left company	—Predecessor remained as chairman
—New president had no prior experience in industry	—New president had no prior experience in industry
($175 million)	($55 million)
Consumer-Products Division	*Industrial- and Office-Products Division*
—Turnaround situation	—Nonturnaround
—Predecessor left company	—Predecessor remained as chairman
—New president had no prior experience in industry	—New president had over twenty-five years' experience in division and industry
($70 million)	($260 million)

only one corporate headquarters. Second, and more important, I could hold potential "headquarter's context" effects as constant as possible. I felt that with a small number of cases and dyads, it would be useful to minimize the potentially idiosyncratic context effects of corporate procedures and requirements that might result from control and budgeting systems, corporate hiring policies, and resource allocation processes. The potential limitation of this decision, of course, was that the findings might be even more site-bound and less able to be generalized than is normal with case studies (McGrath, 1982).

The four cases were selected so that they differed in the degree of situational adversity facing the new presidents and their top management groups. Two divisions were chosen because they were doing well before the succession of the new presidents; the other two because they were in serious economic difficulties and were considered turnarounds by the parent corporation. The assumption behind selecting two "turnarounds" and two "normals" was that the seriousness of the division's problems might affect the pressures on the new president and the nature of his relationships with key subordinates. This contrast ended up being a particularly useful source of variation in studying the taking-charge process although, as I said earlier, it was not part of the original intention.

Another site selection decision was to include one case which was a counter-example in terms of the new president's prior industry-specific and divisional experience. All of the presidents had come from outside of their divisions, although from other assignments within the parent corporation. One, however, had over twenty-five years' experience in his division and had in fact spent most of his career in it before becoming a group officer in another part of the parent (the assignment he had before becoming division president). Although he was new to the division president's job and had been out of the division for three years, he had an intimate knowledge of its products, its industry, and many of its key people. The other three new presidents had no prior experience in their division's industries. For the categories used in this book the counter-example was both an industry and organizational insider, and this contrast proved useful in comparing his actions with that of the others in the speed with which he made changes, the extent of his changes, and the way these differences played themselves out over the three years of the study.

Finally, in two of the divisions, the new president's predecessor was promoted to a chairman's position and remained in the division for the first two years of the study; in the other two sites the predecessors had been fired. It was not possible to use this contrast meaningfully, however, because both sites in which the predecessor remained were nonturnarounds and any comparisons between these two situations and the other two would be confounded by the turnaround versus nonturnaround differences. I had wanted a broader range of industry contexts among the four sites (for example, high-technology, developing industries versus more stable and mature industries) but this proved impossible given the pool of potential sites.

In all four cases, the basis of the new division presidents' promotions was an established track record of success in earlier assignments. Each was considered seasoned and successful by corporate staff before assuming his new post. By the end of the study (three years later) each had also proved successful in his new assignment as judged by his division's economic performance.

ACCESS AND ENTRY TO THE SITES

Finding four new division presidents who were in the same company but who were split in situational adversity essentially meant that I had to approach very large corporations for candidate sites. Only a very large parent would have enough divisions to offer as many as four or five divisions that had recently undergone a change in leadership or were about to undergo such a change. I was fortunate that the first company I approached had five candidate sites that in various combinations would meet my design criteria. My initial contact with the company was arranged with the assistance of a colleague who had consulted to the firm. The company also had been the subject of several Harvard Business School cases and a history of trust and good will existed between the firm and the school. My first official contact in the firm was with a corporate personnel officer who secured permission for me to approach the five division presidents, with the understanding that only they could make the decision to participate.

The first four division presidents I met agreed to participate. The agreement I made with them was that I would not provide counsel or be a sounding board to them during the life of the study, but that I would share my findings with them at its completion. They also agreed that all interview data would be confidential and that I would not give them either opinions or evaluations of their subordinates. The initial "contracting" meetings lasted from one and one-half to two hours. All four presidents asked many questions about the purposes and methods of the study. Two were mildly sceptical about whether my proposed four days of observation of their activities and interactions would yield valid data because of the potential effects of my presence on the behavior of their staffs. One was concerned that people might "play for the camera" and the other was concerned that subordinates might be less open in my presence. I assured both that based on my earlier fieldwork I felt certain that people would quickly be accustomed to my presence and that the normal pressures of business would overcome initial defensiveness or posturing. We also agreed that at the end of the observation period I would ask them for their assessment of what effects, if any, my observation had on people's behavior.

FIELD METHODS

In addition to observation, I collected relevant company documents and held a series of time-staggered interviews with the new presidents, their chairmen, and their key subordinates (defined as all of the new president's direct reports and anyone else within the organization whom he defined as critical to his job).

Observation. Four days of observation were conducted in each site during the first visit. Each four-day period was scheduled in advance based on the new president's judgment that it would comprise a typical segment of four continuous days. This precluded such epicyclical activities as attending a national sales force meeting or an all-day capital appropriation review. The observation was conducted on-site in all four cases except in one instance in which a president spent one of the days visiting a subsidiary in another state. He made three to four such trips a month and felt that the four days should include at least one such trip, especially since a key subordinate was based there.

I patterned my protocol after Mintzberg's (1973) observation of managers at work and made a log for each day, noting the duration of activities and interactions to the nearest minute. At the end of the workday I queried each of the new presidents about interactions I had not understood. My own experience was the same as Kotter's (1982): I needed a great deal of stamina and attention just to keep up with them. This was especially true for two of the presidents who conducted many of their transactions in the hallways or while making tours.

All four introduced me to people as they interacted with them and briefly explained that I was doing a study of general managers taking charge of new assignments. All had also previously described my study to their direct reports before the first site visit.

At the conclusion of the four days, I asked each president what effects my presence had on his behavior or that of subordinates; all agreed that the effects had been minimal. In the sixteen days of on-site observation I was excluded from only two meetings (both at the same site). One was with a senior vice president who was being demoted and the other was with the vice president who was taking his place. The president felt (and I agreed) that these meetings were too personal for a third party to observe. As a practical matter, I also excluded myself from a two-hour board meeting that another president attended at a local bank. With these exceptions, however, I observed each president at work for a continuous four-day period.

Interview Schedules and Protocols.   The time-staggered interviews were designed to yield data points at the 3-, 6-, 12-, 15-, 18-, 24-, 27-, 30-, 36-, and 42-month periods. In addition to this schedule, each new president was interviewed for three hours, before the commencement of fieldwork, to gather background information.

Interviews with the new presidents covered several broad topics: their current concerns and problems; what they had learned about their job and situation since the previous interview; the development of their working relationships with key subordinates; any organizational and personnel changes they were contemplating and the thinking behind these possible changes; and an updating on any organizational, business, or personnel changes that had been made since the last interview. Interviews with the new presidents typically totaled from eight to twelve hours per site visit during the first year of the research, usually spread out over a week. Interviews in subsequent years typically totaled from three to six hours per site visit.

Interviews with key subordinates focused on the same general topics but from the subordinate's point of view and with particular emphasis on the development of their working relationships with the new president. These interviews ranged from two to three hours per site visit in the first year of the study and from one and a half to three hours per site visit in subsequent years.

Finally, I gathered relevant company documents over the three-year period: published organization charts, memoranda on organizational changes, management personnel changes, and "draft" or "bottom drawer" organization charts.

The Ten Historical Studies

The second set of studies consisted of ten successions of general and functional managers in organizations ranging in size from $1.2 million to $3 billion in nine different industries. (See Figure A-3 for a summary of the ten sites.) Unlike the longitudinal studies, these cases were retrospective and involved managers who had been in charge of their assignments for three years, or had been terminated within their first three years of taking charge. The purpose of the historical studies was to attempt to verify, expand on, and qualify the findings of the longitudinal studies.

RETROSPECTIVE VERSUS LONGITUDINAL DESIGN

I decided to use a retrospective rather than a longitudinal design for two reasons. First, longitudinal field studies are enormously labor-intensive, requiring time in the field over a sustained period as well as elapsed time for completion. The findings of the longitudinal studies suggested that from two to two and a half years were needed for a new manager to take charge if one used situational mastery and impact as criteria. It had already been several years since the beginning of the longitudinal studies, and I had little taste for extending the

Figure A-3
Historical Study Site by Business, Revenues, and Position

Business of Unit	Unit Revenues*	Manager's Job
Cable television subsidiary	$1.2 million	General manager
Wholesale food distributor	$21 million	Functional head
District sales service organization (communications)	$30 million	Functional head
Beverage manufacturer	$90 million	General manager
Plastic and metal products	$100 million	General manager
Beverage manufacturer	$110 million	Functional head
Synthetic fibers	$200 million	Functional head
Computer and technical products	$780 million	General manager
Industrial and consumer products	$3 billion	General manager
Public education	(not available)	Functional head

Ten Historical Studies, Break-out by Situational
and Outcome Factors

Outcome of the succession	
Taking charge process was successful	6
Taking charge process was unsuccessful	4
Situational adversity	
Organization doing well before new manager	5
Situation considered a turnaround	5
Responsibility and function of new manager	
General manager	5
Production or operations manager	2
Marketing or sales manager	3
Status of predecessor	
Remained in organization as new manager's superior	3
Left organization	7
Type of Business	
Manufacturing/sales	7
Service operations	3
Location of organization	
U.S.	4
Non-U.S.†	6

*Revenues expressed in 1982 U.S. dollars.
†U.K. (3); Switzerland, Italy, Netherlands

project by another two to three years of fieldwork plus another year of analysis.

A second, and more important, reason for choosing a retrospective design was a concern that some aspects of the first study's longitudinal design might have had a reactive effect on its data. The analysis of the interview and change data in the longitudinal studies had shown a startling degree of periodicity in both the interview themes and in the actions taken by the new presidents. The periodicity and clustering of the changes made by the new presidents were so dramatic that I could not ignore the possibility that it might in some way be a consequence of the time-staggered design I had used in the first set of studies. It was quite possible, for example, that the periodic interviews had provided the new presidents and their subordinates with regularly scheduled opportunities for systematic reflection which they might not have had under normal circumstances, or at least not at scheduled intervals, and that these occasions had, in turn, served to precipitate decisions on changes they had been considering. If this were true, then the changes they implemented would occur in a more periodic fashion than would normally be the case. Under this possibility, the periodicity of the time-arrayed change data could be attributed to researcher-effect (in the form of site visits) rather than to the phenomenon itself.

Clearly, one way to remove any researcher-effect on either learning themes or actions was to study taking charge retrospectively. The three-year point was chosen because, based on the longitudinal studies, I believed that most managers would have taken charge by that time.

COMPARATIVE ASPECTS OF THE DESIGN

The ten cases were chosen to have a comparison of cases along two dimensions: (1) turnarounds versus normals; and (2) successful transitions versus failed successions. I had concluded from the longitudinal studies that whether the situation was a turnaround or a normal succession made a difference on the pressures on the new manager and his people, some of the issues they faced, and the urgency they felt. Although I was quite certain that managers went through the same stages in taking charge, I strongly suspected that in turnarounds the progression was likely to occur more quickly (although the data from the turnarounds in the longitudinal studies did not bear this out). As a result, half the situations chosen were turnarounds and half were not.

I also believed that a comparison of managers who had been successful in taking charge with those who had not would be informative. Since all four of the longitudinal cases had been seen as successful by all parties, I thought that it would be particularly useful to study some situations in which the new manager had failed to take charge effectively. This design decision was based on the belief that much could be learned from a comparative study about behaviors or situational factors that might contribute to success or failure. For this reason, four of the ten historical studies were chosen because they had ended in failure.

The operational difficulties of defining failure and success in taking charge are, on close inspection, permeated with practical as well as epistemological difficulties. I chose a rather primitive, but compelling definition of a failed succession: one in which the new manager was terminated (was fired or quit) within three years of succession for failure to meet performance expectations. This is an operational definition that is open to considerable debate about whether it is a true measure of failure in either mastery or impact, but it had the great virtue of simplicity (it was easy to know one if you saw one) and face validity (a manager could not have been too successful in taking charge if he had been fired for his efforts). The six "successful" cases were situations where the new manager had not been terminated within three years of taking charge; they can be considered typical successions that resulted in varying degrees of success, however one might define the term.

OTHER ASPECTS OF SITE SELECTION

The site selection strategy consisted of first attempting to obtain a mix of cases that would enable comparisons between turnarounds and nonturnarounds and failed and successful transitions, and second, within those broad cuts, to get as much range along the other dimensions as possible. As a practical matter this meant cases were chosen opportunistically to maximize diversity along these dimensions but within the constraints of finding a sample that fit two comparative criteria. No attempt was made to obtain a sample that might be considered in any way random. In fact, the opposite was true in that I intentionally sought cases that would fill "holes" within the total sample as the sample developed.

With success and situational adversity as the primary cuts on the sample, I aimed for as much diversity as possible within the ten sites in terms of other dimensions. These included *type of business* (three in service operations and one of these a public sector organization; seven in more traditional product-based organizations); *type of function* of the new manager (five were general managers and five were functional heads of sales, service, marketing, production, or operations); and *size of the new manager's unit,* with the range extending from a $1.2 million small cable television subsidiary to a $3 billion operating group of a major company. The cases were also chosen for range of diversity in national culture (six of the ten cases came from outside North America).

The decision to include non-American sites resulted directly from the fact that I was working and living in Europe at the time I decided to undertake a second set of studies. The stimulus to thinking about culture as a variable came from a colloquium I gave to the IMEDE faculty in Lausanne on the findings of the longitudinal studies. Several European members were concerned that the strong action patterns found in the longitudinal cases might be artifacts of the American managerial culture. Neither the stimulus nor the possibility of studying non-American sites would have occurred to me had I been in the United States.

The process of searching for sites was also opportunistic: once the first few cases were obtained, I actively sought additional cases that would fill out the design. I used whatever contacts I had, either directly or through former students or business acquaintances, to gain entry and access to potential sites.

ACCESS AND ENTRY

The entry process was much less systematic than for the longitudinal studies. Two of the four failed successions happened in firms where I was already involved in another case-writing project and the access question was relatively easy. In the other two failed successions, I was already acquainted with the two managers and one, in fact, had approached me to discuss the failure. Three of the successful cases occurred in firms that were sponsors of Harvard's International Senior Manager's program; one was in a firm that had been a former client; and the other two cases were sites I had previously studied for other purposes.

METHODS

Methods employed consisted of on-site interviews and the gathering of relevant documents about structural changes, personnel changes, policy statements, and memoranda on other significant changes (the creation of product policy task forces, for example). The site visits lasted from one to three days depending on the number of people who could be interviewed and the difficulty of obtaining archival data. In two cases, it was not possible to retain relevant documents because they were considered proprietary and confidential by the companies. In one case this meant borrowing confidential documents for three months and in another it meant extracting and recording relevant information from company records while at the site.

The Three Supplementary Studies

These three case studies were of general management successions in units with revenues of $80 million, $500 million, and $650 million, in the plastics, heavy equipment, and computer industries respectively. Their purpose was to supplement the first fourteen cases by further grounding and explicating the dilemmas and tasks identified in the findings of the first two sets of studies. The three supplementary studies were conducted at the invitation of a large U.S. corporation as part of an executive development and planning effort for high potential senior management candidates.

The cases were chosen for a range of unit size and industry. The first two cases were studied retrospectively at the six-month and two-year periods. The third case was studied longitudinally over three years at the 6-, 18-, 20-, 30-, and 36-month periods. The longitudinal site was especially interesting to me and the company because it involved a situation which the findings of the first two studies suggested would be particularly difficult.

Fieldwork consisted of interviews with the new managers and their subordinates and the gathering of documents concerning strategic, organizational, product and personnel actions. The data gathered in the supplementary studies are used in this book for illustration only and are not included in any of the aggregated or disaggregated change results because only one of the three sites was studied for a full three years. The aggregated change data and activity profiles presented in chapters 2 and 3, therefore, do not include the three supplementary studies and are based only on the first fourteen cases.

A summary of salient characteristics of all seventeen sites is given in Table 1-1, chapter 1.

B

OTHER RESEARCH STUDIES

Although no single prior study has examined all of the facets of taking charge, several have a bearing. The purpose of this review is to summarize research relevant to taking charge and to connect the present study to this larger body of work.

Putting the Topic in Perspective

The process of taking charge can be considered the culmination of a management succession. Unlike the larger topic of management succession, however, very little empirical or field research has been done on the actual activities and processes that managers perform.

The few exceptions include two landmark field studies of successions: Gouldner's (1954) study of a new manager of a gypsum plant; and Guest's (1962a) study of a new manager of an automobile plant. Gouldner examined the bureaucratic patterns initiated by the new manager as a result of institutional pressures and the consequences of his actions. Guest's study looked at changes in leadership patterns and their consequences for plant morale and productivity. Both studies, despite their age, remain robustly descriptive and are still rich with insights about the dynamics of taking charge. Most other work on the taking-charge process per se, however, is largely prescriptive rather than descriptive or is based on anecdotal data or personal experience (see, for example, Bibeault, 1982; Goodman, 1982; Bennis and Nanus, 1985).

In contrast, a great deal of research has been done on the conditions *leading* to successions and the situational, background, and personal factors influencing them. Although these studies have not focused on the taking-charge process per se, they have considerable relevance for understanding how managers take charge, the problems they are likely to face, and their eventual success.[1] In addition, several recent studies of managerial learning are also relevant to the learning, assessment, and diagnostic work of taking charge as well as to the patterns of learning and action described in this book.

Effects of the New Manager's Background and Experience

The management succession literature is relatively rich in research on the effects of background on a new manager's actions and the problems he or she is likely to face. Unfortunately, much of this work pertains to corporate chief executive officers rather than senior-level general managers or functional managers, and it is not clear that all of the findings are applicable to my studies.

ORGANIZATIONAL INSIDERS VERSUS ORGANIZATIONAL OUTSIDERS

Most empirical work on the effects of a new manager's background has focused on differences between managers promoted from within (organizational insiders), and those brought in from outside (organizational outsiders). The findings concerning successions at the CEO level are quite consistent: organizational outsiders tend to replace more subordinates and make more changes than insiders. In a widely cited study of school system superintendents, Carlson (1962) found that organizational outsiders, whom he characterized as career-bound and mobile, instituted more organizational changes than organizational insiders, whom he described as place-bound and long-tenured.

Carlson argued that organizational outsiders (because of their orientations and predispositions) are more task-oriented than insiders; that outsiders, because they are not part of the existing political system, face more neutral and cooperative staffs than insiders. This enables them to expand their staffs, building a base of "beholden" supporters, thereby enabling them to retool the organization for a new direction. Carlson also theorized that an outsider effectively suspends the social system of interest groups and cliques, which gives him greater flexibility and latitude in ameliorating internal conflict and in redirecting the organization's course.

Studies by Grusky (1960) and by Helmich (1971) and his colleagues support the presence of this pattern among CEO successions in the United States. An important study by Helmich and Brown (1972) tested Grusky's earlier findings that inside successions (in their case to corporate presidencies) resulted in fewer replacements of subordinates than did outsider successions. In this major study of 208 chemical and allied product companies, they found that organizational outsiders made more personnel changes among their "executive role constellations" (Hodgson, Levinson, and Zaleznik, 1965) than insiders. Helmich and Brown found this pattern to persist even when controlled for successor style, firm performance, size, growth, and base technology. Helmich (1975b) also found that older firms tended to promote insiders more often than outsiders. Later studies by Helmich (1977a, 1977b) supported his earlier findings and also showed that outsider CEOs were more likely to expand the size of their boards concurrent with their replacement of vice presidents. He found, however, that rapid rates of turnover at the top tend to slow the pace of organizational growth.

These strong and persistent findings appear on first blush to be inconsistent with those in this book—*industry* insiders initiate much more change than industry outsiders. There are several factors that help explain this apparent contradiction. First, the Carlson, Grusky, and Helmich studies pertained to differences between *organizational* insiders and organizational outsiders, while the findings here concern differences between *industry* insiders (defined as having five or more years of experience in the industry of the new assignment), and industry outsiders. Industry outsiders and organizational outsiders are not the same. It is likely that many if not most of the organizational outsiders in the CEO successions studied by Helmich and Brown were insiders to their industries. Indeed, a study by Peery and Shetty (1976) of new CEOs in twenty-six different industry groups supports this contention. Less than 5 percent of their CEOs had come from other industries.

Second, Helmich studied CEO rather than senior-level executive successions. In appointing a new CEO, the decision to search outside the firm is very likely a reflection of an explicit desire by a board to bring about change. Thus, we would expect outsider CEOs to actively initiate more change than insiders. Brady and Helmich (1984) make this point in discussing Carlson's earlier research: "In extrapolating this theory to general organizational situations we might conclude that outside-elected successors are typically brought in because of the need for substantial change" (p. 48). They make the same point in reference to CEO aspirations following succession: "The outside CEO successor is typically brought in with a mandate for change and this invariably entails firing or pressuring members of the executive staff into leaving" (p. 50).

INDUSTRY-RELEVANT EXPERIENCE AND TRANSFERABILITY OF SKILLS

Unfortunately, very little research has been done on the effects of industry-specific experience per se on either the degree of change a new manager makes or on the success of that change. The little research that has been done on the transferability of an executive's skills across industries suggests that transferability is limited. Peery and Shelty (1976) found that of 270 corporations in twenty-six different industry groups only 29 had gone outside of their firms for executives in the top-level category and only 14 of these were industry outsiders. Brady and Helmich (1984) cite this study in describing the costs involved for industry outsiders in taking charge, underscoring the difficulty and amount of time needed for an industry outsider to acquire the "organizational and institutional skills (knowledge of the intricate pattern of interaction of the firm with key elements of the environment)" that are needed to take charge (pp. 107–108).

Their conclusions are consistent with Kotter's research on general managers and the importance of industry and institutional knowledge to their effectiveness (Kotter, 1982, 1985). Brady and Helmich also discuss some of the problems industry outsiders face, including difficulties in overcoming opposition and gaining acceptance. They indicate that outsiders report more problems in being unprepared and in lacking knowledge about the firm or industry than do insiders. These conclusions support my own conclusions about the importance of prior industry-specific experience at upper levels and the difficulties the new manager faces in taking charge when this industry experience is lacking.

PRIOR FUNCTIONAL EXPERIENCE

Unfortunately, there is almost no research within the management succession literature on the effects of prior functional experience. The only study cited in Brady and Helmich's exhaustive review concerns differences in the leadership style tendencies of young managers with different functional backgrounds. In another study, Hall (1976) found that companies generally had CEOs with backgrounds in the company's general category of technology. Firms in technologically sophisticated industries tended to have CEOs with technical backgrounds, while those involved in technologically unsophisticated industries tended to draw CEOs with marketing and sales experience. The inference is that firms choose CEOs with functional backgrounds appropriate to their firms' needs, but the study did not describe how this prior experience influenced CEOs' actions as they took charge.

Although not specifically focusing on the effects of prior functional experience, Salancik and Pfeffer (1977), in a study of hospital administrators, confirmed Thompson's (1967) work on the relationship between succession to leadership and a candidate's ability to cope with organizational uncertainties. They concluded that managers "are selected to cope with the organization's critical contingencies, and . . . these contingencies are related to organizational context" (p. 75). One of the inferences of this influential study is that some backgrounds will be seen as more salient than others, depending on the particular problems or challenges an organization faces. One would also expect that new managers who possess the skills needed to deal with critical contingencies would start with stronger power bases and perhaps also stronger mandates for change (Pfeffer, 1981).

In summary, the strongest findings concerning the effects of a manager's background pertain to differences between the amount of change made by organizational outsiders and that made by those promoted from within. The clear theme in this research is that outsider CEOs make more personnel and organizational changes than insider CEOs. These findings are qualified by the premise that boards go outside to choose CEOs when they want change and that organizational outsiders therefore begin with a stronger change mandate than insiders. Very little research has focused on the effects of prior industry-specific experience, but the work that has been done suggests strongly that at senior levels, industry-specific experience is an important variable and that the transferability of certain organizational and institutional skills across industry settings is low. Although the research on this topic is meager, it is strongly consistent with the findings reported in chapter 5.

Situational Factors in Management Successions

The two most extensive reviews of situational and contextual factors bearing on successions are given by Gordon and Rosen (1981) and Brady and Helmich (1984).

GORDON AND ROSEN (1981): SITUATIONAL FAVORABLENESS

In a detailed synthesis of the post-Weber literature on succession, Gordon and Rosen posit a "situational favorableness" model that is particularly exhaustive in terms of internal contextual factors bearing on a succession. Their model consists of twenty organizational factors that can be inventoried to predict the likely effectiveness of a successor. These include the goal motivation of the group to be led; the legacy of the predecessor; flexibility of the group's role structure; cohesion and conformity within the group; level of democratization within it; and the existence of irreversible policies that may be in the newcomer's path.

The factors Gordon and Rosen identified largely refer to the firm's internal context rather than to external contingencies, but they provide a means for gauging how difficult an internal situation a new manager is likely to face. For the issues covered in this book, they are indicators of how much organizational and interpersonal work is needed to take charge effectively as well as how difficult this work is likely to be, as described in chapters 4 and 5.

BRADY AND HELMICH 1984: INTERNAL AND EXTERNAL CONTEXT

In another exhaustive review of the succession literature, Brady and Helmich identify a number of situational variables that are likely to influence the difficulties faced by a new manager. These include the situational adversity of the firm's performance; the severity of the specific problems facing the new CEO; the allies available to him; and the size and stability of the organization's management staff. Discussing "successions in rough times," they argue that it is difficult to change CEOs in the midst of organizational problems and that the break in leadership in management change will only exacerbate these problems, especially if the new CEO is an outsider. Although their arguments are not based directly on empirical work, they are consistent with the findings in chapter 3 which describe the difficulties and urgency facing managers taking charge of turnarounds as well as the learning and credibility tasks facing industry outsiders. The relationship Brady and Helmich posit between the size and stability of the new manager's executive group and the difficulties he is likely to face also have implications for the amount of both interpersonal and organizational work needed to take charge. For the present research, these internal factors can be considered predictors of how difficult and critical the relationship and team-building work described in chapters 4 and 5 are likely to be.

There is some further evidence that whether or not the assignment is a turnaround will also influence the difficulty the new manager faces in taking charge. Brady and Helmich, for example, cite work by Grusky (1961), and Ginzberg and Reilly (1961), showing that managers taking charge of organizations experiencing performance problems face a high degree of instability and unrest among their executive ranks. This cannot help but make the team-building and relationship-development tasks described in chapters 4 and 5 more difficult. In addition, Brady and Helmich's comments about the interpersonal difficulties of taking charge during "rough times" also support the findings in chapter 3 on the importance of developing effective working relationships with one's superiors and key subordinates during the first twelve months of taking charge. Finally, their observations are consistent with the findings in the present research that turnaround managers experience a more heightened sense of urgency than those in nonturnarounds, and have to deal with greater levels of fear on the part of their subordinates.

There is also a considerable body of research that suggests that poor performance is itself a cause of management succession, but that frequent changes in management have an adverse influence on organizational performance over the long run (Gordon and Rosen).[2] In his classic study of managerial change in baseball teams, Grusky (1961) showed that (1) rates of succession and degree of prior organizational effectiveness were negatively correlated, and (2) rates of change in leadership were negatively correlated with subsequent change in performance. Using a different analysis, Gamson and Scotch (1964) disputed his interpretation and argued that changes in team leadership were really scapegoating rituals. They saw the team manager's impact on performance as minimal. In reply, Grusky (1964b) partitioned his sample into insider versus outsider successions and showed that insider successions did have an effect on performance while outsider successions did not, at least not for the first season. Allen, Panian, and Lotz (1979) also found that frequent successions of managers were negatively related to team performance but that the variable accounted for only a small percentage of the variance.

Brady and Helmich, citing a study by Brown (1982) conclude that the relationship between performance and succession goes both ways: that although ritual scapegoating may occur, organizations having performance problems will, for common sense reasons alone, be more likely to change leadership than those which do not; but that continuous changes in leadership can be a source of decreased performance over the long run because of the disruption that these changes cause.

Other contextual factors concerning situational adversity which have been found to influence either the frequency of management changes or difficulties facing new managers taking charge—at least at the CEO level—include changes in board membership and a firm's debt-to-equity ratio (Helmich, 1978) and, at a more basic level, how well a firm is structurally prepared for major strategic reorientations (Brady, Helmich, and Moore, 1983).

SUCCESSION ITSELF AS A SOURCE OF DISRUPTION

Although there is some disagreement in the literature about the relationship between succession and performance, there is little controversy over succession itself being a cause of both disruption and difficulty. Whatever the longer-term consequences of a succession, a change in management is a source of destabilization and disruption, at least in the short term. This observation was first made by Gouldner and Grusky (1959), and again by Grusky (1960) building on the work of Weber (1946), Gouldner (1954), and Newcomer (1955). Gouldner and Grusky argued that successions are sources of major disruptions in the organization as a whole and in the executive role system in particular. A field experiment by Jackson (1953) confirms the disruptive consequences of changes in leadership. More recently, Brady and Helmich also describe successions as destroying group cohesiveness and engendering conflict. They cite early studies by Whyte (1948), Dale (1957), and others which document increased levels of tension, resignations, and other dramatic events (including arson) as negative consequences of successions.

The inherent social disruption caused by successions may be one reason why a new manager's ability to develop effective working relationships discriminates so strongly between the failed and successful successions reported in chapter 3. Also the need to create a focused and unified management group in the wake of a change in leadership may be one reason why the organizational and interpersonal work described in chapters 4 and 5 is so critical to taking charge effectively.

OTHER SITUATIONAL FACTORS

Brady and Helmich have also identified the board's composition and its support as factors influencing a new CEO's difficulties in taking charge. Although their observations concern CEOs and are beyond the scope of the senior-level management successions studied in the present research, they nonetheless highlight the importance of support from superiors during and prior to the new manager's taking charge. Also identified as important situational factors are the role and strategy of one's predecessor in terms of contrast effect (Gordon and Rosen, 1981); the presence of allies who will bridge between the new manager and his successor (Brady and Helmich, 1984); and a predecessor's attempts to impede changes initiated by the new manager (McGovern, 1978), especially if predecessors remain as major shareholders in entrepreneurial firms (Christensen, 1953). Concerning the potentially subversive effects of one's predecessor, Levinson (1974) goes so far as to warn incumbent CEOs against handpicking their successors. He argues that unconsciously CEOs wish to prove that no one can fill their shoes and therefore they will choose replacements who are likely to fail or, at a minimum, perform less well than they had. Although predecessor resistance as such did not emerge as a major factor in my cases, it is a variable that should be borne in mind when assessing potential problems in taking charge.

In summary, a number of situational factors can influence the difficulties faced by a manager taking charge. These include situational adversity in terms of existing performance problems as well as specific problems the new manager must deal with. They also include support from superiors, size and stability of staff, allies in the top management group (particularly those who can help bridge the transition from the predecessor to the new manager), the predecessor himself, and the favorableness of the situation in terms of receptivity to a new manager and changes he might make (as described, for example, in Gordon and Rosen's situational favorableness model).

Effects of Management Style and Preferences

My research suggests that a new executive's management style and preferences for control or delegation can influence not only how he takes charge but also some of the structural changes he makes. Although the effects of management style on succession has not been studied widely, some evidence supports my findings. How a new manager's style affects the actions he takes are well documented in two of the earliest case studies of management successions. Gouldner (1954) described in detail the consequences of a new plant manager's impersonal and bureaucratic style, including noncooperation and a "lionizing" of his predecessor who had been strangely unloved while he was in command (which Gouldner labeled the "Rebecca Myth" after the lamented figure in Daphne du Maurier's novel). The new manager "strategically replaced" key people as a means of reducing resistance and further bureaucratizing the organization. Gouldner's findings were consistent with an earlier study by Argyris (1952) cited in Brady and Helmich. Argyris found that within five months of succession, new managers with bureaucratic styles caused greater turnover in lower supervisory ranks than did those with participative styles.

Guest (1962a, 1962b) also stressed the effects of a new manager's leadership style on the actions taken by a new plant manager and their consequences. In contrast to Gouldner's study, the new plant manager in Guest's study established informal personal ties with subordinates and, ignoring the bureaucratic procedures and powers vested in his office, elicited workers' views on how to improve performance through informal networks. Guest (1962b) outlined the parallels and differences between the managers he and Gouldner studied and attributed the success of his manager to an open, informal, people-centered leadership style. (This study has since become a classic in both the succession and leadership literature.) Koch (1962) examined the adaptation of plant supervisors to a new head of operations whose style was highly structured and found patterns of dissatisfaction similar to Gouldner's (1954) study that had supported Guest's (1962b) conclusions.

Subsequent work, however, has not supported the clear dichotomy in the effects of task-centered styles and people-centered styles on performance that Gouldner and Guest advanced. Kotin and Sharaf (1967) have characterized the advantages and disadvantages of these two styles in terms of "tight" and "loose" approaches to taking charge. A "tight" style is desirable when it enables an administrator to impose order and controls on a situation that is dysfunctionally ambiguous or chaotic. They argue that a "loose" style is effective when it is desirable to maintain flexibility, such as when the organization's work requires creativity or when it is desirable for the new manager to leave a situation intentionally ambiguous, for example, when a manager wishes temporarily to avoid confronting conflict or to buy time as he establishes himself. Kotin and Sharaf further argue that these stylistic predispositions also influence the structural and direct-influence actions a new manager attempts. Kotin and Sharaf's conclusions are consistent with the findings in chapter 3 and the descriptive data in chapters 4 and 5.

Hemlich has also contributed to this topic. Several of his surveys and actuarial studies have focused explicitly on the potential effects of management style. In developing a model of presidential succession, Helmich (1975a) concludes that a new manager's "need deficiency" is the most important variable influencing his actions, including how task-oriented he is likely to be (consistent with earlier work by Carlson, 1962). He also predicts that task-oriented leaders will deemphasize interpersonal relationships and induce or create subordinate turnover. On the other hand, he also found evidence in another study that the more employee-centered the new CEO, the more he tended to make changes in executive staff positions (Helmich, 1975c). Less clear is the relationship between leadership style and performance. Although Helmich (1971) earlier found that the CEO's employee-centered style was somewhat associated with profitability, he was reluctant to generalize from these findings because of the low degree of association.

Based on this and other research, Brady and Helmich make several conjectures about the effects of leadership style but conclude that the advantages of one style over another are highly situational, depending on the need for creativity and the maturity of an organization, and that success or failure is not so much dependent on the style of influencing as it is on the appropriateness of that style to the power context.

In summary, studies on the effects of a new manager's preferences and style on a management succession suggest that these variables influence a new manager's actions in taking charge. Although none has dealt directly with the hands-on versus delegatory dimension that emerged in the present research, it should not be surprising that this dimension also is reflected in actions taken and that it can surface as a source of conflict in management styles.[3]

The Work of Taking Charge

In some respects, the last empirical studies to probe the actual activities of new managers, *as they take charge,* are the classic field studies of Gouldner (1954) and Guest (1962a, 1962b). Since then, most work on the taking-charge process itself has tended to be prescriptive rather than descriptive and has been based on either anecdotal evidence or personal experience rather than on empirical research (e.g., Bibeault, 1982; Goodman, 1982). Some recent work has focused on broad leadership processes (Bennis and Nanus, 1985) such as the leader's vision, his ability to empower an organization, and his creation of meaning (see, in particular, Bennis and Nanus, pp. 26–84, 89–109; and 215–226). Other work such as Steiner (1983) has focused on the work of formulating public policy, dealing with constituent interest groups, and the social performance and responsibility issues facing the new CEO.

Nonetheless, several studies of managerial succession are relevant to the organizational and interpersonal work described above.

GORDON AND ROSEN: POSTARRIVAL FACTORS

Perhaps the work that bears most directly on the organizational and interpersonal activities of taking charge treated in this book are the postarrival factors described by Gordon and Rosen (1981). In their comprehensive review of the literature on management succession Gordon and Rosen synthesize earlier work by using a prearrival-postarrival model of succession. Their treatment of prearrival factors covers many of the variables and studies reviewed earlier in this Appendix concerning situational, contextual, and background factors. Of particular interest here is their review of work related to what managers do *after* they have assumed an assignment and, more important, Gordon and Rosen's own conceptualization of what comprises these activities.

Specifically, Gordon and Rosen review and synthesize a number of empirical studies relevant to the process of taking charge including the classic Gouldner and Guest studies (see pp. 228–237; pp. 246–250). In addition, they cite several laboratory studies by Grusky (1969a, 1969b) on the use of allies in successions, and by Hamblen (1958) on the effects of crises in enhancing a new leader's influence, which are both germane to understanding a new manager's potential sources of power and consistent with the findings reported in chapter 3. They also review several experimental field studies, including work by Rosen (1969) showing the importance of a new manager's ability to re-establish equilibrium after taking charge as well as some of the changes that result in group performance patterns after changes in leadership have stabilized (Rosen, 1969, 1972). Also relevant to the work of taking charge is a longitudinal study they cite by Lieberman (1956), which posits that new managers placed in an unfamiliar role will tend to take on or develop expectations associated with that role.

Of far more immediate importance, however, is Gordon and Rosen's own concept of postarrival factors. In conceptualizing these factors, they go significantly beyond the studies they review (or any I have read). They identify three postarrival factors which deal "with aspects of the succession that occur after the successor has formally assumed his or her position and is physically located on the job." Each factor refers to a range of activities which, in my view, are germane to the organizational and interpersonal work of taking charge.

The three postarrival factors they posit are:

1. *Mutual observation* in which the new manager and his group check each other out for the accuracy of perceived or expected characteristics. This process includes comparisons of the new manager and his predecessor and what Gordon and Rosen call getting acquainted—the sending, receiving, and evaluating of role expectations for both sides that set the stage for future action.
2. *The new manager's actions and reactions,* which includes how the new manager copes with the immediate problem of gathering information, how the new manager establishes himself, and how he handles discrepancies between his perceptions of goals and those of others.
3. *The development of sources of power and influence,* which includes sources of power the new manager is perceived as having before assuming the role as well as how he develops or acquires sources of power as he takes charge.

If these postarrival factors are considered activities involved in taking charge, they are consistent with the findings in chapters 4 and 5. For example, the "mutual observation" factor is closely related to the early orientational assessment and diagnostic work described in chapter 4 and the orientational and mutual exploration tasks described in chapter 5. The activities described by Gordon and Rosen as "sending, receiving, and evaluating role expectations" is closely related to the early work of developing a set of shared expectations. Similarly, the activities they subsume under the "new manager's actions and reactions" factor is also germane to the organizational tasks described in chapter 4 of working through differences in expectations and developing a cohesive management team. Finally, "development of power and influence" is directly related to the interpersonal work pertaining to the development of expectations, influence, and trust and their relationship to a new manager's credibility.

OTHER STUDIES

Several other studies are also relevant to the organizational and interpersonal work described in this book. McGivern (1978), in a study of successions in two small firms, identified several tasks as critical to a new manager's success in taking charge. These include the tasks of (1) gaining control, (2) developing an appropriate leadership style, (3) building effective working relationships, and (4) developing technical skill and knowledge relevant to the assignment.[4] Similarly, in a review of succession issues in the mental health field, Greenblatt (1983) identified two key postarrival phases as critical to the effectiveness of a succession: (1) the assertion of the new leader's personality, style, and programs; and (2) the working through of differences. Both phases include activities related to the work of developing shared expectations and the building of effective working relationships. According to Greenblatt, these phases of a succession are uncomfortable and conflict-laden and often require changes in a subordinate's role or performance expectations. He concludes that the new leader must "work through" many stubborn problems and resistances and this dynamic process of resolution rivals anything that goes on in psychotherapy even with clients who possess the most intransigent defenses.

Stages of Learning and Action

To my knowledge, there is no other research that has studied the stages of learning and action that characterize the taking-charge process. Evidence exists, however, that managers learn as a result of their past experience and apply that knowledge to new situations (McCall and Lombardo, in press; Frys, 1975; Cooper, 1979; Davies, 1984; Zemke, 1985). There is also evidence that managers learn as they engage new situations (Moore 1969, 1974; Leavitt, 1972; McKenny and Keen, 1974; Kolb, 1974; Tongh, 1979; Chorba, and New, 1980), and are capable of using that learning to adapt to and act on new situations (Kolb, 1976; Burgoyne and Hodgson, 1983; Kolb, Rubin, and McIntyre, 1974, 1984).

MANAGERIAL LEARNING AND ACTION

The stages and the patterns of periodicity of learning and action presented in chapter 2 are, I believe, manifestations of underlying learning processes that are beyond the scope of the present research, its design, or methods. They can, nonetheless, be explained post hoc by existing concepts of managerial learning. One can safely postulate that managers learn from the process of taking on a new assignment (Tongh, 1979; Davies, 1984), act on that learning (Kolb et al., 1984), and receive feedback from their actions, which further enhances their learning (Leavitt, 1972; Burgoyne and Hodgson, 1983). The enhanced learning in turn becomes the basis for further, but more informed action (Burgoyne and Hodgson, 1983; Kolb and Rubin, 1984). Although I believe this is a basic dynamic underlying the three-wave pattern and the stages presented in chapter 2, it does not explain why the wave pattern dampens out by the twenty-seven-month period. It may simply be the manager eventually exhausts his "newness" so that continued situational learning becomes progressively incremental and routine, once a new manager has acquired an in-depth understanding.

Several speculations can be made about the differences in the learning in different stages. It is possible, for example, that the Taking-Hold stage (which coincides with the first wave of documented action), corresponds to a period of concrete experience and active experimentation (in Kolb et al terms) but little double-loop learning (in Argyris and Schön, 1974, terms) because the manager is so pressed by the exigencies of grasping the new situation. The Immersion stage, which corresponds to the trough between the first and second waves of action, clearly involves more reflection (Schön, 1983; Kolb et al, 1984). Reflective observation, one can argue, leads to abstract conceptualization by the end of the stage, as well as more double-loop learning—at least for effective executives—because the period provides an opportunity to learn from the actions of the Taking-Hold stage and to examine underlying assumptions. Seen in these terms, the heavily action-oriented Reshaping stage, which coincides with the second wave of action, is a period of active experimentation *and* concrete observation, which exploits the more reflective learning of the Immersion stage. The final stage, Consolidation, corresponding to the second trough and the third wave, is likely to involve the entire range of learning from concrete experience (early in the stage) to active experimentation (late in the stage).

I would suspect that the degree to which double-loop learning occurs, as defined by Argyris and Schön, would be more a result of the new manager himself than of the particular stage he is in, regardless of the greater opportunities that some stages might offer for such learning.

OTHER STAGE PARADIGMS

Although no previous research has explicitly explored the stages of learning and action in taking charge, several authors have posited or described activity stages. Redlich (1977) has the following stages of succession:

1. *Anticipatory stage*: a period of uncertainty and anxiety until a new manager is chosen.
2. *Appointment stage*: the successor is announced, thereby relieving some anxiety; information is exchanged about him; the reality of the succession sets in.
3. *Inauguration stage*: superiors assure constituents that all will be well; a show of solidarity and optimism.
4. *Honeymoon period*: a period of sizing up, testing out, and learning; successor tries to make a good impression.
5. *Assertion of new leader's personality, style, and programs*: a period of discomfort, disagreement in which differences emerge.
6. *Working through of differences*: a period of resolution of differences and stabilizing relationships with key norm-setting individuals.
7. *Establishment of equilibrium*: a new equilibrium is established and new norms are set.

Redlich's stages 4 and 5 would coincide with the Taking-Hold stage described in chapter 3, and his stage 6 might continue into the Immersion period, but would be unlikely to last longer than this stage in successful transitions. Unfortunately, a new manager is likely to work through the kinds of activities Redlich described at different rates with different subordinates, and therefore these activities do not correspond exactly to the stages described in chapter 2.[5]

Bibeault (1982) also described several stages of taking charge: (1) Choosing a Strategy; (2) Getting People's Attention; (3) Dealing with Immediate Actions; (4) Attacking Problems. These stages do not correspond to those I have identified except as they might be generally descriptive of the initial learning and action in the first stage, Taking Hold.

Finally, Morrison (1975) described three stages of management succession, two of which are prearrival. The third stage includes "the problems of taking control and introducing change, developing an appropriate leadership style, building effective working relationships, handling continuing influence from the retired chief executive, and the development of the successor's technical and management skill and knowledge."[6] These activities would pertain to Taking Hold, Immersion, and Reshaping and are mainly relevant to the organizational and interpersonal work of taking charge rather than to the stages of learning and action.

Notes

1. Two of the most comprehensive and integrated reviews of management succession literature can be found in Brady and Helmich (1984) and Gordon and Rosen (1981). Both reviews begin with the early post-Weber work of Gouldner (1954), Gouldner and Grusky (1959), and Grusky (1960), and continue to the present.
2. Other situational factors related to the decision to change leadership and rate of succession, but not reviewed here, include size of firm and degree of bureaucratization (Grusky, 1961, 1964a; Kriesberg, 1962; Gordon and Becker, 1964; Gordon and Rosen, 1981).
3. I should note that Brady and Helmich (1984) view a "hands-on" approach as a task-oriented form of leadership (pp. 168–169).
4. McGivern (1978) identifies these activities within a stage framework developed by Morrison (1975) which consists of: (1) Recognition of need for succession; (2) Selection of successor and exit of predecessor; and (3) Activities after formal succession.
5. This discussion is based on a review of these stages given by McGivern (1983) based on Redlich, "Problems of Succession and Administrative Style," presented at Annual Meeting, American Psychiatric Association, Toronto, 1977.
6. Quoted from McGivern (1978).

APPENDIX

C

ACTIVITY DATA AND ORGANIZATIONAL CHANGE MEASURES

This appendix describes the sources of the activity data referred to in chapter 4, summarizes these data in tabular arrays, and explains the conventions used in operationalizing the organizational change data in chapters 2 and 3.

Organizational Activity Data

The primary source for both the change and activity data in this book was the case chronologies (described in Appendix A), consisting of time-sequenced records of major actions taken by the new managers during their first three years in office. Information summarized in the case chronologies included: structural and personnel changes made; the introduction or modification of information or control systems; the initiation of task forces or problem-focused committees; the initiation of recurrently scheduled meetings (such as production or product review meetings); the introduction of performance appraisal systems; changes in compensation systems influencing a major or minor subunit of the organization; the initiation of strategic reviews such as a divisional strategy review or a market strategy analysis; and major confrontations that occurred between the new managers and a subordinate or superior.

As described in Appendix A, the case chronologies were constructed based on data from interviews, internal memoranda, and other company documents. In the longitudinal case studies, these data were gathered over three years according to the time-staggered design given in Appendix A. In the retrospective studies, the data were gathered post hoc for the first three years of the manager's tenure except for the failed successions in which they were gathered retrospectively for whatever length of time the manager had been in the job before termination. As would be expected, the chronologies for the longitudinal studies were more detailed and extensive than those developed for the retrospective studies.

Table C-1 summarizes the organizational activities initiated by new managers in the longitudinal case studies for the first six months, second six months, second year, and third year. The activities are broken out in five broad categories: (1) Entry activities (explicitly

Table C-1

Organizational Activity Initiated by Time Period (Longitudinal Studies)

Activity	Cases			
I Entry Activities	Case 1	2	3	4
• Orientational meetings with direct reports	①	①	①	①
• Formal group briefings or reviews (as orientation)			①	①
• Tours or site visits	①	①	①	①
II Meetings				
• Problem-focused meeting (not recurrently scheduled)	①②③④	①②③④	①②③④	①② ③④
• Schedules formal group meetings (recurrently scheduled)		① ④		①
• Schedules one-to-one meetings (recurrently scheduled)		①		
III Management Systems				
• Institutes or revises budgeting system		①	①	②
• Institutes or changes information system	②	①	①②③	①
• Institutes or changes control system	②	① ③	① ③	①②③
• Institutes or changes planning system		①	①	
• Institutes or changes performance appraisal system	③	① ③	③④	②③
• Establishes problem-focused task forces or committees	②	① ③	②	①
• Establishes strategic review or analysis process			④	
• Establishes internal training or development programs				①
• Establishes or alters personnel hiring practices		①		①
• Institutes changes in compensation system	③		③	
IV Organization Structure				
• Structural changes envolving two or fewer minor subunits	① ③	①	③	① ③
• Structural changes involving two or fewer major subunits	① ③	③	① ③	① ③
• Structural changes involving entire organization	①	③	③	
• Creates new organization subunit or function not previously existing	①	②③	①②	①
V Management Personnel Changes				
• Terminates management personnel			①② ④	
• Initiates search for new mangement person		①②③	② ④	③
• Hires or promotes management personnel	①②③	②③④	②③	① ③
• Reassigns management personnel (lateral)	①②③	③		

① First 6 months, ② Second 6 months, ③ Second year, ④ Third year orientational); (2) use of meetings; (3) use of systems; (4) changes in organizational structure; and (5) changes in management personnel. Table C-2 provides a more detailed reporting by case and time period of the specific activities initiated by the new managers in each of the four longitudinal cases. Table C-3 gives a comparative summary of the kinds of activities engaged in by new managers in both the longitudinal and retrospective studies during their first eighteen months of taking charge.

Organizational Change Measures

The change data in chapters 2 and 3 are based on a composite measure of structural and personnel changes. These two component measures were used because each was comparable across cases using a common set of conventions (described below) and because each could be reduced to a common metric that could be aggregated within or across cases. None of the other activity or change data contained in the case chronologies could meet these criteria. For example, although it was possible to "count" changes in information and control systems and the frequency of introduction of task forces, the extensiveness and impact of these changes varied greatly across cases and even within cases. Any attempts to aggregate such data as indicators of change would have been meaningless. Moreover, even if such changes in systems and practices had been comparable, they seldom left a documentary trail, making it difficult to pinpoint their introduction to a specific month (unlike personnel and structural changes which were normally announced in memoranda). The ability to find a documentary trace was particularly important in the historical studies, for they were retrospective. In contrast, changes in structure or personnel were traceable post hoc to a specific month.

Thus none of the activity data given in the case chronologies except those pertaining to personnel and structural changes was used either for measuring change or for comparative purposes, except in the form of simple descriptive summaries such as those given in Tables C-1, C-2, and C-3.

Conventions Used in Operationalizing Personnel Changes

The following conventions were used to devise a common metric for operationalizing changes in management personnel:

Case	First 3 Months	4 to 6 Months	7 to 12 Months	Second Year	Third Year
(1) Industrial and Office Products Division	• Structural changes affecting international manufacturing, controller, and EDP • Reorganizes division from functional to geographic organization • No formalized task forces or committees • Extensive 1:1 ad hoc and problem-focused (nonrecurrent) problem-oriented meetings	• Ad hoc task force on potential divestiture • Ad hoc task force on management information systems • Extensive scheduled visits to sales districts and key customers	• Transfers VP out of division; hires replacement • Implements changes in information and control systems • Ad hoc task force on sales compensation	• Restructures domestic marketing and sales organization • Change in sales organization compensation system • Extended tour of sales districts (explaining changes) • 10 related personnel changes in division management • Above includes 2 hires and 8 transfers within division • Divestiture of plant and product line	• Oversees continued implementation of MIS • No further structural or systems changes
(2) Machine tool division	• Functionalizes one of the product divisions • Institutes weekly production scheduling meetings on all orders (½ day) • Institutes formalized hiring approval procedure • Extensive tours of plants	• Early retirement of marketing VP • Dissuades engineering VP from early retirement • Centralizes engineering for all but one product division • Engages consulting firm to assist in doing an organization study	• Creates tooling and systems design group reporting to VP operations • Completes reorganization study	• Reorganizes division from product to functional structure except for division "defunctionalized" in first 3 mos., which is now reconstituted as a product group • Promotes internally 3 people to VPs • Hires new director of manufacturing reporting to VP operations	• Stops chairing weekly production scheduling meetings • Initiates weekly staff meetings of division officers • Hires VP engineering

(continued)

Table C-2
Organizational Activities—First Three Years (Longitudinal Studies)
(continued)

Case	First 3 Months	4 to 6 Months	7 to 12 Months	Second Year	Third Year
	• Institutes formal weekly meetings with each direct report • Initiates changes in manufacturing, information, and control systems	• Extensive tours of plants • Creates task force on inventory control and materials management • Initiates performance appraisal system for direct reports • Broadens and deepens scope of quarterly and annual profit plans and budgeting systems • Initiates search for new VP marketing		• Creates VP of project management position • Changes implemented in materials and inventory control systems • Initiates performance appraisal system for all exec.-level personnel • Initiates task force on spare parts pricing, control, and sales. • Initiates search for VP engineering	
(3) Consumer Products Division	• Fires controller; hires replacement • Extensive 1:1 meetings with direct reports • Ad hoc, problem-focused meetings • Implements reduction in overhead • Initiates design of a standard cost system • Tightens purchasing system	• Terminates president of product group • Functionalizes above group so all department heads report to him directly • Curtails autonomy and responsibility of product development • Implements "project management" system • Institutes quarterly performance progress meetings • Creates cost management function	• Terminates VP of sales; initiates search • Adds a creative director for function reporting to product development • Implements an inventory costing system • Changes policy on special order pricing • Changes policy on receivables • Initiates ad hoc task force on pricing	• Reorganizes division from product to functional organization with exception of one subsidiary • Hires new VP marketing • Consolidates and reorganizes marketing and sales for all products • Initiates new compensation systems and policy for sales • Implements new control system for marketing	• Initiates discussions concerning potential merger • Fires controller • Begins strategic review • Implements performance appraisal system • Initiates search for director of strategic planning • Initiates revision of costing system in manufacturing

(continued)

Table C-2

Organizational Activities—First Three Years (Longitudinal Studies)

(continued)

(4) Construction Products Division	• Creates position of production control manager • Initiates daily production meetings • Revises process for 5-year plan • Initiates comprehensive manufacturing scheduling system • Makes extensive plant tours (which continue for duration of study)	• Institutes new product line review procedure, changing final responsibility from product development to marketing • Reduces product line • Reorganizes manufacturing by product lines • Institutes weekly executive staff meetings • Implements new hiring and salary approval system • Initiates program to re-evaluate manufacturing standards • Expands and revises MPS facilities and systems • Expands scope of business review and budgeting process • Establishes credit committee • Institutes daily phone report system on per-shift product figures and shipments • Implements management development program	• Moves product development under market and sales VP • Implements cost reduction program • Changes performance appraisal system	• Reorganizes engineering by product lines • Controller quits, hires replacement • Restructures administration and finance function • Reorganizes personnel function • Modifies performance appraisal system to include MBO system • Implements comprehensive quality control system	• [No changes in structure or systems]

Table C-3

Summary of Organizational Activities Initiated During First 18 Months

Case:	General Manager Successions									Functional Manager Successions				
	1	2	3	4	5	6	7	8	9	10	11	12	13	14
I Entry Activities														
• Orientational meetings with direct reports	X	X	X	X	X	X	X	X	X	X	X	X	X	X
• Formal group briefings			X								X			
• Tours or site visits	X	X	X	X	n.a.	X		X	X	X	n.a.	X	X	X
II Meetings														
• Initiates formally scheduled recurrent meetings		X		X	X	X			X			NA	X	
• Initiates formally scheduled one-to-one meetings		X										NA		
III Management Systems														
• Initiates changes in information/control systems	X	X	X	X	X	X	X	X	X		X	X	X	
• Establishes problem-focused task forces or committees	X	X	X	X			X	X	X					X
• Initiates strategic analysis or review process	X					X		X	X	X				X
IV Organization Structure														
• Initiates changes involving two or fewer subunits	X	X	X	X	X	X	X	X	X	X		X	X	n.a.
• Initiates changes involving three or more subunits	X	X	X					X	X				X	n.a.
V Management Personnel Actions														
• Terminates management personnel			X			X	X	X	X	X				X
• Hires or promotes management personnel	X	X	X	X	X	X		X	X	X	X	X	X	X
• Reassigns management personnel	X	X	X	X	X	X		X	X	X	X	X	X	X

X = action initiated.
NA = data not available.
n.a. = action not applicable.

1. Only changes involving personnel in the top three levels of the new manager's organization were counted. This convention was used to limit the relevant population as the organizations varied greatly in size and in the number of management levels—from as few as three to as many as six. The assumption in limiting the relevant field is that the three levels comprise the leadership of the organization and that changes made in these ranks would have comparable effects in organizations regardless of their size.
2. A personnel change was defined as being any personnel action which resulted in a termination, promotion, or reassignment within the top three levels of the organization.
3. All personnel actions occurring within the top three levels were equally weighted as personnel changes, regardless of whether it was a promotion, reassignment or termination, or the level of the job.
4. A personnel action was counted as occurring during the month in which it was officially announced, regardless of when the new manager had actually decided to make the change.

Conventions Used in Operationalizing Structural Changes

The following conventions were used in constructing a common metric for counting structural changes:

1. Only structural changes involving major and minor subunits of the new manager's organization were counted.
2. Major subunits were defined as being either major functional units which reported directly to the new manager or major product organizations which reported directly to him. Examples of major functional units include manufacturing, sales, engineering, or R&D organizations reporting directly to the new manager. Examples of major product organizations include product divisions or product groups reporting directly to the new manager.
3. Minor subunits were defined as either staff units reporting directly to the new manager (such as the controller's department, a separate MIS, or personnel department that reported to him), or departments or divisions which comprised the next level below the major subunits that reported directly to him (such as the manufacturing department of a product division that reported to him).
4. A change in the structure of a minor subunit was counted as one

unit of structural change. A change in the structure of a major functional subunit was counted as two units of structural change, and a change in the structure of a major product subunit was counted as three units of structural change.

5. A structural change was counted as occurring during the month in which it was officially announced, regardless of when the new manager might actually have decided to make the change.

Time Arraying the Change Data

Using these conventions, it was possible to provide some summary indicators of changes in structure and management personnel by three-month periods for each case. If, for example, a manager had changed the structure of his controller's department (one subunit), reorganized his sales division (two subunits), and fired his vice president of manufacturing and replaced him with an outside hire (two personnel actions) during his second three months in office, the changes he initiated during this period would be two personnel actions and three units of structural change.

Time-arrayed summaries of both structural and personnel changes were constructed for each case site using these conventions. Examples of these time-arranged histograms are given in Figure C-1, which provides summaries of organizational changes made by three-month periods for each of the longitudinal cases.

The conventions described above also allow the personnel and structural changes to be reduced to common metrics of units of structural change and personnel actions. With this assumption of commonality it was possible to aggregate data by time period across cases. Figure C-2 presents summary histograms of both structural and personnel changes made in the longitudinal cases by three-month periods. Figure C-3 presents this data in percentage form for all of the completed successions by six-month periods. Finally, Figure C-4 presents the duration of each stage for the four longitudinal case studies using the operational definitions given in chapter 2.

Composite Change Measure

The purpose of the composite change measure was to combine in one indicator the degree of both personnel and structural changes made within a given period. In this respect, I attempted to devise an indi-

Figure C-1
Summary of Organizational Changes for Each Case, Longitudinal Studies

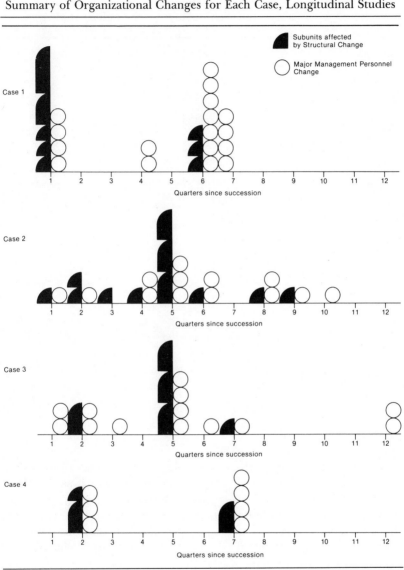

Figure C-2
Distribution of Activities by Three-Month Periods Since Taking Charge
and Approximate Duration of Stages, Longitudinal Studies

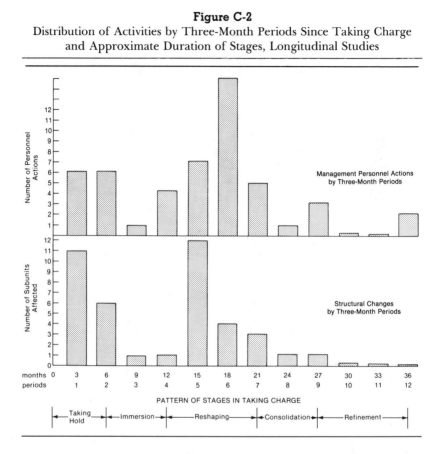

cator that enabled me to display in one array data what would otherwise require two separate displays or histograms (such as those presented in Figure C-2). As such, the composite change measure is a
synthetic indicator, unlike the personnel and structural change data
presented in Figure C-2 or the individual case data presented on
Figure C-1 which are based on first order measures of change.

The composite measure was arrived at by computing the average
number of structural and personnel changes made per period for the
sample and then simply adding these two figures on a per period
basis. The additionality assumption was made as a matter of conven-
ience so that a single summary measure of organizational change

Figure C-3
Personnel and Structural Changes Made by Six-Month Periods

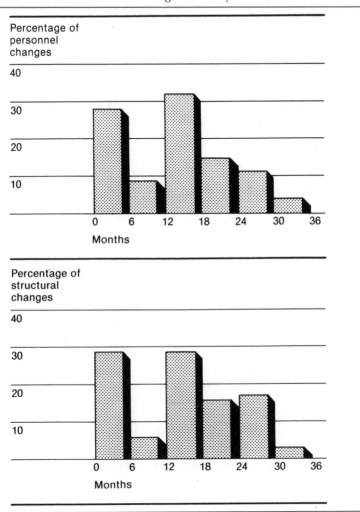

Figure C-4
Duration of Stages, Longitudinal Studies
(Lengths of each stage given in months)

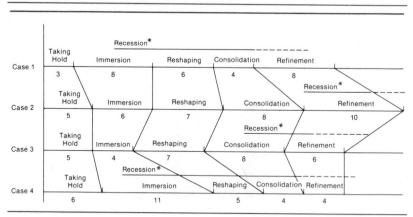

*Industry recession.

could be used. No pretense is made that the two component measures are of the same type or of comparable impact. On the other hand, each of the component measures is a valid indicator of change (and of dislocation and turbulence, as the research reviewed in Appendix B suggests), and the composite measure does provide a cumulative indicator of both types of changes on a per period basis.

In computing the composite change measure, only data from the ten completed successions were used (those successions in the longitudinal and retrospective studies in which the new manager lasted in the job for thirty months or longer). The same sample was used in computing the data presented in Figure C-3, on the average percentage of structural and personnel change made per period.

SELECTED BIBLIOGRAPHY

Allen, M., Panian, S., and Lotz, R. "Managerial Succession and Organizational Performance: A Recalcitrant Problem Revisited." *Administrative Science Quarterly,* June 1979, *24* (2), 167–180.

Altman, I. "The Communication of Interpersonal Attitudes: An Ecological Approach." In T. L. Huston (Ed.), *Foundations of Interpersonal Attraction.* New York: Academic Press, 1974.

Altman, I., and Taylor, D. A. *Social Penetration: The Development of Interpersonal Relationships.* New York: Holt, Rinehart, and Winston, 1973.

Argyris, C. *Executive Leadership.* New York: Harper and Brothers, 1952.

———. "The Executive Mind and Double-Loop Learning." *Organizational Dynamics,* 1982, *11* (2), 5–22a.

———. *Increasing Leadership Effectiveness.* New York: Wiley-Interscience, 1976.

———. *Interpersonal Competence and Organizational Effectiveness.* Homewood, Ill.: Dorsey Press, 1962.

———. *Reasoning, Learning, and Action: Individual and Organizational.* San Francisco: Jossey-Bass, 1982b.

Argyris, C., and Schön, D. *Theory in Practice: Increasing Professional Effectiveness.* San Francisco: Jossey-Bass, 1974.

Athos, A. G., and Gabarro, J. J. *Interpersonal Behavior.* Englewood Cliffs, N.J.: Prentice-Hall, 1979.

Barnes, L. B. "Managing the Paradox of Organizational Trust." *Harvard Business Review,* March-April 1981.

Bennis, W., and Nanus, B. *Leaders: The Strategies for Taking Charge.* New York: Harper and Row, 1985.

Bennis, W. G., and others. *Interpersonal Dynamics.* Homewood, Ill.: Dorsey Press, 1964.

Bernstein, P. W. "Going Outside Can Be Dangerous." *Fortune,* 1980, *124* (3), 185–186.

Berscheid, E., and Walster, E. *Interpersonal Attraction*. Reading, Mass.: Addison-Wesley, 1968.

Biddle, B. J., and Thomas, E. J. *Role Theory: Concepts and Research*. New York: Wiley, 1966.

Brady, G. F., Fulmer, R. M., and Helmich, D. L. "Planning Executive Succession: The Effect of Recruitment Source and Organizational Problems on Anticipated Tenure." *Strategic Management Journal*, 1982, *3* (3), 269–275.

Brady, G. F., and Helmich, D. L. *Executive Succession Toward Excellence in Corporate Leadership*. Englewood Cliffs, N.J.: Prentice-Hall, 1984.

Brady, G. F., Helmich, D. L., and Moore, J. N. "The Comparative Advantage of Variation Among Diversified and Non-Diversified Firms," *Proceedings of the Eastern Academy of Management*, Annual Meeting, Pittsburgh, 1983.

Brown, M. C. "Administrative Succession and Organizational Performance: The Succession Effect." *Administrative Science Quarterly*, 1982, *27* (2) 1–16.

Burgoyne, G., and Hodgson, V. E. "Natural Learning and Managerial Action: A Phenomenological Study in the Field Setting." *Journal of Management Studies* (U.K.), 1983, *20* (3), 387–399.

Carlson, R. D. *Executive Succession and Organizational Change*. Danville, Ill.: Interstate Printers and Publishers, 1962.

Chorba, R. W., and New, J. L. "Information Support for Decision-Maker Learning in a Competitive Environment: An Experimental Study." *Decision Sciences*, 1980, *11* (4), 603–615.

Christensen, C. R. *Management Succession in Small and Growing Enterprises*. Boston: Division of Research, Harvard Business School, 1953.

Cooper, C. L. *The Executive Gypsy: The Quality of Managerial Life*. London: Macmillan, 1979.

Dale, E. "DuPont: Pioneer in Systematic Management." *Administrative Science Quarterly*, 1957, *2* (1), 25–59.

Dalton, G., Barnes, L. B., and Zaleznik, A. *The Distribution of Authority in Formal Organizations*. Boston: Division of Research, Harvard Business School, 1968.

Davies, J., and Easterby-Smith, M. "Learning and Developing from Managerial Work Experiences." *Journal of Management Studies* (U.K.), 1984, *21* (2), 169–183.

Denzin, N. *The Research Act: A Theoretical Introduction to Sociological Methods*. New York: McGraw-Hill, 1970.

Derlega, V. J., and Grzelak, J. "Appropriateness of Self-Disclosure." In G. J. Chelune (Ed.), *Self-Disclosure*. San Francisco: Jossey-Bass, 1979.

Deutsch, M. "Cooperation and Trust: Some Theoretical Notes." *Nebraska Symposium on Motivation*. Lincoln: University of Nebraska Press, 1962, 275–319.

Donnelly, K. J. "The Assimilation Process at General Electric." Presented at the Annual Meeting, Academy of Management, San Diego, 1985.

Dubin, R., and Spray, S. L. "Executive Behavior and Interaction." *Industrial Relations*, 1964, *3*, 99–108.

Eitzen, D. S., and Yetman, N. "Managerial Change, Longevity, and Organizational Effectiveness." *Administrative Science Quarterly*, 1972, *17*, 110–116.

Farris, G. F., and Lim, F. G., Jr. "Effects of Performance on Leadership, Cohesiveness, Influence, Satisfaction, and Subsequent Performance." *Journal of Applied Psychology*, 1969, *53*, 490–497.

Foy, N. "Action Learning Comes to Industry." *Harvard Business Review*, September–October 1977, 58–68.

Friedman, S. D. "Succession Systems and Organizational Performance in Large Corporations." Dissertation, University of Michigan, 1984.

Gabarro, J. J. "Socialization at the Top: How CEOs and Their Subordinates Evolve Interpersonal Contracts." *Organizational Dynamics*, Winter 1979, 3–23.

———. "The Development of Trust, Influence, and Expectations." In A. G. Athos and J. J. Gabarro (Eds.), *Interpersonal Behavior*. Englewood Cliffs, N.J.: Prentice-Hall, 1978.

———. "The Development of Working Relationships." In J. W. Lorsch, *Handbook of Organizational Behavior*. Englewood Cliffs, N.J.: Prentice-Hall, 1986.

———. "Stages in Management Succession: The Process of Taking Charge," *Course Development and Research Profile*. Boston: Harvard Business School, 1983.

Gabarro, J. J., and Kotter, J. P. "Managing Your Boss." *Harvard Business Review*, January-February 1980, 92–100.

Gamson, W., and Scotch, N. "Scapegoating in Baseball." *American Journal of Sociology*, 1964, *70*, 69–70.

Gephart, R. P. "Status Degradation and Organizational Succession: An Ethnomethodological Approach." *American Sociological Quarterly*, 1978, *23* (4), 553–581.

Ginzburg, E., and Reilly, E. W. *Effecting Change in Large Organizations*. New York: Columbia University Press, 1961.

Glaser, B., and Strauss, A. L. *The Discovery of Grounded Theory: Strategies for Qualitative Research*. Chicago: Aldine, 1967.

Goodman, S. J. *How to Manage a Turnaround*. New York: Free Press, 1982.

Gordon, G., and Becker, S. "Organizational Size and Management Succession: A Reexamination." *American Journal of Sociology*, 1964, *70*, 215–222.

Gordon, G. E., and Rosen, N. "Critical Factors in Leadership Succession." *Organizational Behavior and Human Performance*, 1981, *27*, 227–254.

Gouldner, A. W. "The Problem of Succession in Bureaucracy." In Robert Merton (Ed.), *Reader in Bureaucracy*. Glencoe, Ill.: Free Press, 1952.

———. "Succession and the Problem of Bureaucracy." *Patterns of Industrial Bureaucracy*. Glencoe, Ill.: Free Press, 1954. Also in O. Grutzy and G. A. Miller (Eds.), *The Sociology of Organizations: Basic Studies*. New York: Free Press, 1970.

———. *Patterns of Industrial Bureaucracy*. Glencoe, Ill.: Free Press, 1954.

Gouldner, A. W., and Grusky, O. "Role Conflict in Organizations: A Study of Prison Officials." *Administrative Science Quarterly*, 1959, *3* (4), 463–467.

Gray, B., Bougon, M. G., and Donnellon, A. "Organizations as Constructions and Destructions of Meaning." *Journal of Management,* 1985, *11* (2), 83–98.

Greenblatt, M. "Management Succession: Some Major Parameters." *Administration in Mental Health,* 1983, *11* (1), 3–10.

Grusky, O. "Administrative Succession in Formal Organizations." *Social Forces,* 1960, *39* (2), 105.

———. "Corporate Size, Bureaucratization, and Managerial Succession." *American Journal of Sociology,* 1961, *67*, 263–269.

———. "Effects of Inside vs. Outside Succession on Communication Patterns." *Proceedings of the 77th Annual Convention of the American Psychological Association,* 1969, 451–452.

———. "The Effects of Succession: A Comparative Study of Military and Business Organizations." In M. Janowitz (Ed.), *The New Military.* New York: Russell Sage Foundation, 1964. Also in O. Grusky and G. A. Miller (Eds.), *Sociology of Organizations: Basic Studies.* New York: Free Press, 1970.

———. "Managerial Succession and Organizational Effectiveness." *American Journal of Sociology,* 1963, *69*, 21–31. Also in A. Etzioni (Ed.), *A Sociological Reader in Complex Organizations.* 2d ed. New York: Holt, Rinehart, and Winston, 1969.

———. "Reply (to 'Scapegoating in Baseball')." *American Journal of Sociology,* 1964, *70*, 72–76.

———. "Succession with an Ally." *Administrative Science Quarterly,* 1969, *14*, 155–170.

Guest, R. H. *Organizational Change: The Effect of Successful Leadership.* Homewood, Ill.: Irwin-Dorsey, 1962.

———. "Managerial Succession in Complex Organizations." *American Journal of Sociology,* 1962, *68*, 47–54.

Guiot, J. M. "Attribution and Identity Construction: Some Comments." *American Sociological Review,* 1977, *42*, 692–704.

Hall, J. L. "Organizational Technology and Executive Succession." *California Management Review,* 1976, *19* (1), 35–39.

Hamblin, R. "Leadership and Crises." *Sociometry,* 1958, *21*, 332–335.

Hayes, R., and Abernathy, W. "Managing Our Way to Economic Decline." *Harvard Business Review,* July-August 1980, 67–72.

Helmich, D. L. "The Executive Interface and President's Leadership Behavior." *Journal of Business Research,* 1975, *3* (1), 43–52.

———. "Executive Succession in the Corporate Organization: A Current Integration." *American Management Review,* 1977, *2* (1), 252–266.

———. "Corporate Succession: An Examination." *Academy of Management Journal,* 1975, *3*, 429–441.

———. "Organizational Growth and Succession Patterns." *Academy of Management Journal,* 1974, *17*, 771–775.

———. "The Impact of Administrative Succession on the Executive Role Constellation." Dissertation, University of Oregon, 1971.

———. "Organizational Volatility and Rate of Leader Succession: The Effect of Recruitment Source and Organizational Problems on Anticipated Tenure." *Strategic Management Journal,* 1982, *3* (3), 269–275.

———. "Predecessor Turnover and Successor Characteristics." *Cornell Journal of Social Relations,* 1974, 249–260.

———. "The President's Position: Successor Characteristics and the Organizational Process." *University of Michigan Business Review,* 1977, *29* (1), 11–14.

———. "Succession: A Longitudinal Look." *Journal of Business Research,* 1975, *4,* 355–364.

———. "Subordinates' Desirability of Leaving and President's Promotional Origin." *Akron Business and Economics Review,* 1976, 7 (2), 45–49.

Helmich, D. L., and Brown, W. B. "Successor Type and Organizational Change in the Corporate Enterprise." *Administrative Science Quarterly,* 1972, *17,* 371–381.

Hinde, R. A. "On Assessing the Bases of Partner Preferences." *Behavior,* 1977, *62,* 1–9.

———. "Some Problems in Study of Development of Social Behavior." In E. Tobach, L. R. Aronson, and E. Shaw (Eds.), *The Biopsychology of Development.* New York: Academic Press, 1971.

———. *Towards Understanding Relationships.* London: Academic Press, 1979.

Hodgson, R. C., Levinson, D. J., and Zaleznik, A. *The Executive Role Constellation: An Analysis of Personality and Role Relations in Management.* Boston: Division of Research, Harvard Business School, 1965.

Huston, T. L. *Foundations of Interpersonal Attraction.* New York: Academic Press, 1974.

Jacobson, W. D. *Power and Interpersonal Relations.* Belmont, Calif.: Wadsworth, 1972.

Jones, E. E., and Archer, R. L. "Are There Special Effects of Personalistic Self-Disclosure?" *Journal of Experimental Social Psychology,* 1976, *12* (2), 180–193.

Jones, E. E., and Goethals, G. R. "Order Effects in Impression Formation: Attribution Context and the Nature of the Entity." In E. E. Jones, and others (Eds.), *Attribution: Perceiving the Causes of Behavior.* Morristown, N.J.: General Learning Corp., 1972.

Jones, E. E., and Gordon, E. M. "Timing of Self-Disclosure and Its Effects on Personal Attraction." *Journal of Personality and Social Psychology,* 1972, *24* (3), 358–365.

Jones, E. E., and Thibaut, J. W. "Interaction Goals as Bases of Inference in Behavior." In R. Tagiuri and L. Petrullo (Eds.), *Person Perception and Interpersonal Behavior.* Stanford, Calif.: Stanford University Press, 1958.

Jourard, S. M. *Self-Disclosure: An Experimental Analysis of the Transparent Self.* New York: Wiley-Interscience, 1971.

———. "Self-Disclosure and Other Cathexis." *Journal of Personality and Social Psychology,* 1959, 59. ff.

Kerckhoff, A. C. "The Social Context of Interpersonal Attraction." In T. L.

Huston (Ed.), *Foundations of Interpersonal Attraction*. New York: Academic Press, 1974.

Koch, J. L. "Managerial Succession in a Factory and Changes in Supervisory Leadership Patterns: A Field Study." *Human Relations*, 1978, *31* (1), 49–58.

Kolb, D. A. "On Management and the Learning Process." In Kolb, and others (Eds.), *Organizational Psychology: A Book of Readings*. 2d ed. Englewood Cliffs, N.J.: Prentice-Hall, 1974a.

———. "Management and the Learning Process." *California Management Review*, 1976, *18* (3), 21–31.

Kolb, D. A., and Fry, R. "Towards an Applied Theory of Experiential Learning." In C. L. Cooper (Ed.), *Theories of Group Processes*. London: Wiley, 1975.

Kolb, D. A., Rubin, I. M., and McIntyre, J. M. *Organizational Psychology: An Experiential Approach*. 2d ed. Englewood Cliffs, N.J.: Prentice-Hall, 1984.

Kolb, D. A., and Wolfe, D. M. "Career Development, Personal Growth, and Experiential Learning." In D. A. Kolb, and others (Eds.), *Organizational Psychology: Readings on Human Behavior in Organizations*. 4th ed. Englewood Cliffs, N.J.: Prentice-Hall, 1984.

Kotter, J. P. *The General Managers*. New York: Free Press, 1982.

———. "Power, Dependence, and Effective Management." *Harvard Business Review*, July-August 1977, 125–136.

———. *Power and Influence*. New York: Free Press, 1985.

Kriesberg, L. "Careers, Organization Size, and Successions." *American Journal of Sociology*, 1962, *68*, 355–359.

Lawless, D. J. *Effective Management: A Social Psychological Approach*. Englewood Cliffs, N.J.: Prentice-Hall, 1972.

Leavitt, H. *Managerial Psychology*. 3d ed. Chicago: University of Chicago Press, 1972.

Levinger, G. "A Three-Level Approach to Attraction: Toward an Understanding of Pair Relatedness." In T. L. Huston (Ed.), *Foundations of Interpersonal Attraction*. New York: Academic Press, 1974.

Levinson, H. "Don't Choose Your Own Successor." *Harvard Business Review*, November-December 1974, 53–62.

Liden, R. C., and Graen, G. "Generalizability of the Vertical Dyad Linkage Model of Leadership." *Academy of Management Journal*, September 1980, *25*, 451–465.

Lieberman, S. "The Effects of Changes in Roles on the Attitudes of Role Occupants." *Human Relations*, 1956, *9*, 385–402.

Lowin, A., and Craig, J. R. "The Influence of Level of Performance on Managerial Style: An Experimental Object-Lesson in the Ambiguity of Correlational Data." *Organizational Behavior and Human Performance*, 1968, *3*, 440–458.

Luke, R. A., Jr. "Managing as Learning." *Training and Development Journal*, 1984, *35* (8), 24–30.

Martin, J. "A Garbage Can Model of the Research Process." In J. McGrath, J.

Martin, and R. A. Kulka (Eds.), *Judgement Calls in Research*. Beverly Hills: Sage Publications, 1982.

McCaskey, M. B. "Place Imagery and Nonverbal Cues." In A. G. Athos and J. J. Gabarro (Eds.), *Interpersonal Behavior*. Englewood Cliffs, N.J.: Prentice-Hall, 1978.

McGivern, C. "The Dynamics of Management Succession." *Management Decision* (U.K.), 1978, *16* (1), 32–42.

McGrath, J. "Dilematics: The Study of Research Choices and Dilemmas." In J. McGrath, J. Martin, and R. A. Kulka (Eds.), *Judgement Calls in Research*. Beverly Hills: Sage Publications, 1982.

McGrath, J., Martin, J., and Kulka, R. A. "Some Quasi Rules for Making Judgement Calls in Research." In J. McGrath, and others (Eds.), *Judgement Calls in Research*. Beverly Hills: Sage Publications, 1982.

———. (Eds.). *Judgement Calls in Research*. Beverly Hills: Sage Publications, 1982.

McKenney, J. L., and Keen, P. G. W. "How Managers' Minds Work." *Harvard Business Review*, May-June 1974, 79–90. In H. J. Leavitt, and others (Eds.), *Reading in Managerial Psychology*. 3d ed. Chicago: University of Chicago Press, 1980.

Mintzberg, H. "Managerial Work: Analysis from Observation." *Management Science*, 1971, *18* (2), B97–B110.

———. *The Nature of Managerial Work*. New York: Harper and Row, 1973.

Moore, M. L. "Managerial Learning and Socialization." Dissertation, University of Michigan, 1969.

———. "Superior, Self, and Subordinate Differences in Perceptions of Managerial Learning Times." *Personnel Psychology*, 1974, *27* (2), 297–305.

Morgan, G. "Exploring Choice: Reframing the Process of Evaluation." In G. Morgan (Ed.), *Beyond Method: Strategies for Social Research*. Beverly Hills: Sage Publications, 1983.

Newcomer, M. *The Big Business Executive: Factors that Made Him, 1900–1950*. New York: Columbia University Press, 1955.

Osborne, R. N., and others. "The Event of CEO Succession: Performance and Environmental Conditions." *American Management Journal*, 1981, *24* (1), 183–191.

Peery, N. S., and Shetty, Y. K. "An Empirical Study of Executive Transferability and Organizational Performance." *Academy of Management Proceedings*, University of Colorado, 1976, 145–149.

Pfeffer, J. *Power in Organizations*. Marshfield, Mass.: Pitman, 1981.

Posner, B. Z., and Munson, J. M. "The Impact of Subordinate-Supervisor Value Consensus." *Akron Business and Economic Review*, 1979, *10* (2), 37–40.

Redlich, F. C. "Problems of Succession." Presented at Annual Meeting, American Psychiatric Association, Toronto, 1977.

Rosen, N. *Leadership Change and Work Group Dynamics*. Ithaca, N.Y.: Cornell University Press, 1969.

———. "Open Systems Theory in an Organizational Sub-System: A Field

Experiment." *Organizational Behavior and Human Performance*, 1970, *5*, 245–265.

Ross, J., and Ferris, K. R. "Interpersonal Attraction and Organizational Outcomes: A Field Examination." *Administrative Science Quarterly*, 1981, *26* (4), 617–632.

Rubin, Z. "Disclosing Oneself to a Stranger: Reciprocity and Its Limits." *Journal of Experimental Social Psychology*, 1975, *11* (3), 233–260.

Salancik, G. R., and Pfeffer, J. "Organizational Context and the Characteristics and Tenure of Hospital Administrators." *Academy of Management Journal*, 1977, *20* (1), 74–88.

———. "Effects of Ownership and Performance on Executive Tenure in U.S. Corporations." *Academy of Management Journal*, 1980, *23* (4), 653–664.

Sathe, V. *Managerial Action and Corporate Culture.* Homewood, Ill.: Richard D. Irwin, 1985.

Scott, C. L. III. "Interpersonal Trust: A Comparison of Attitudinal and Situational Factors." *Human Relations*, 1980, *33*, 805–812.

Secord, P. F., and Backman, C. W. *Social Psychology.* New York: McGraw-Hill, 1964.

Sgro, J. A., and others. "Perceived Leader Behavior as a Function of the Leader's Interpersonal Trust Orientation." *Academy of Management Journal*, 1980, *23* (1), 161–165.

Steiner, G. A. *The New CEO.* New York: Macmillan, 1983.

Stewart, R. *Choices for the Manager: A Guide to Managerial Work and Behavior.* London: McGraw Hill, 1982.

———. *Managers and Their Jobs.* London: Macmillan, 1967.

Tagiuri, R. "Person Perception." In G. Lindzey and E. Aronson (Eds.), *Handbook of Social Psychology.* Reading, Mass.: Addison-Wesley, 1969.

Tagiuri, R., and Petrullo, L. *Person Perception and Interpersonal Behavior.* Stanford, Calif.: Stanford University Press, 1958.

Tedeschi, J. T. "Attributions, Liking, and Power." In T. L. Huston (Ed.), *Foundations of Interpersonal Attraction.* New York: Academic Press, 1974.

Thibaut, J., and Kelley, H. H. *The Social Psychology of Groups.* New York: John Wiley and Sons, 1959.

Thomas, R. "Managing the Psychological Contract." In P. Lawrence, L. Barnes, and J. Lorsch (Eds.), *Organizational Behavior and Administration.* Homewood, Ill.: Richard D. Irwin, 1976.

Thompson, J. D. *Organizations in Action.* New York: McGraw-Hill, 1967.

Tolman, E. C. *Behavior and Psychological Man.* Berkeley: University of California Press, 1951.

Tongh, A. *The Adult's Learning Projects.* 2d ed. Austin: Learning Concepts, 1979.

Triandis, H. C. *Interpersonal Behavior.* Monterey, Calif.: Brooks-Cole, 1977.

Valenzi, E., and Dessler, G. "Relationships of Leader Behavior, Subordinate Role Ambiguity, and Subordinate Job Satisfaction." *Academy of Management Journal*, 1978, *21* (4), 671–678.

Van Maanen, J. "Introduction." In J. Van Maanen, J. Dabbs, Jr., and R. Faulkner (Eds.), *Varieties of Qualitative Research*. Beverly Hills: Sage Publications, 1982.

———. "Reclaiming Qualitative Methods for Organizational Research: A Preface." In J. Van Maanen (Ed.), *Qualitative Methodology: An Updated Reprint of the December 1979 Issue of Administrative Science Quarterly*. Beverly Hills: Sage Publications, 1983.

———. (Ed.). *Qualitative Methodology: An Updated Reprint of the December 1979 Issue of Administrative Science Quarterly*. Beverly Hills: Sage Publications, 1983.

Wall, J. A., and Adams, J. S. "Some Variables Affecting a Constituent's Evaluations of and Behavior Toward a Boundary Role Occupant." *Organizational Behavior and Human Performance*, 1974, *2*, 290–408.

Walton, R. E. *Interpersonal Peacemaking: Confrontations and Third-Party Consultation*. Reading, Mass.: Addison-Wesley, 1969.

Walton, R. E., and others. *Social and Psychological Aspects of Verification, Inspection, and International Assurance*. Lafayette, Ind.: Purdue University Press, 1968.

Weber, M. *From Max Weber: Essays in Sociology*. Edited by H. H. Gerth and C. W. Mills. New York: Oxford University Press, 1946.

Weick, K. E. *The Social Psychology of Organizing*. 2d ed. Reading, Mass.: Addison-Wesley, 1979.

———. "Systematic Observational Methods." In G. Lindzey and E. A. Aronson (Eds.), *The Handbook of Social Psychology*. Reading, Mass.: Addison-Wesley, 1968.

Weiss, H. M. "Social Learning of Work Values in Organizations." *Journal of Applied Psychology*, 1978, *63* (6), 711–718.

Wexley, K. N., and others. "Attitudinal Congruence and Similarity as Related to Interpersonal Evaluations in Manager-Subordinate Dyads." *Academy of Management Journal*, 1980, *23* (2), 320–330.

Whyte, W. F. "The Social Structure of the Restaurant Industry." *American Journal of Sociology*, 1949, *54* (4), 302–310.

Wortman, C. B., and Linsenmeier, J. A. W. "Interpersonal Attraction and Techniques of Ingratiation in Organizational Settings." In G. Salancik and B. M. Stow (Eds.), *New Directions in Organizational Behavior*. Chicago: St. Clau Press, 1977.

Wortman, C. B., and others. "Self-Disclosure: An Attributional Perspective." *Journal of Personality and Social Psychology*, 1976, *33* (2), 184–191.

Zemke, R. "The Honeywell Studies: How Managers Learn to Manage." *Training*, August 1985, 46–51.

INDEX